MILLER'S MANUAL

A Research Guide to the Major
French-Canadian Genealogical Resources
What They are and How to Use Them

Tanguay - Jetté - Drouin - PRDH
Loiselle - Tanguay Abbreviations
Baptism, Marriage and Burial Records -
Common Terms and Abbreviations and
an Historical Time Line

By

Douglas J. Miller

**French-Canadian Interest Group
Southern California Genealogical Society**

QUINTIN PUBLICATIONS

1st Printing, February 1997
2nd Printing, August 1997

Quintin Publications, Inc.
28 Felsmere Avenue, Pawtucket, Rhode Island. 02861-2903
(401) 723-67-97
Fax (401) 726-0327
www.quintinpublications.com
bobquint@aol.com

ISBN: 1-886560-47-1

A complete catalog listing hundreds of titles on Canadian genealogy and history is available free upon request.

Table of Contents

THE TANGUAY

THE TANGUAY

What is the Tanguay ?

The proper title for this French Canadian research resource is **Dictionnaire Généalogique des Familles Canadiennes** or Genealogical Dictionary of Canadian Families. The seven volumes were compiled by Reverend Cyprien Tanguay, a Catholic priest, and originally published between 1871 and 1890. It is called the " Tanguay" .

The Tanguay is a "genealogical dictionary" as opposed to a mere recitation of baptismal, marriage, or burial records. It is presented in alphabetical order in the format of family genealogies (family notices), which flow from generation to generation.

Reverend Tanguay published his first volume in 1871 and it contains only families whose marriages took place during the period from the beginning of the French colony *circa.* 1608 to 1700. This first volume included the entire alphabet A to Z.

Six additional volumes were published over the next 20 years. These volumes begin with the letter A in Volume 2 and end with the letter Z in Volume7 and cover the period 1700 to 1760. Some families are carried down to the 19th century but this is not too common.

These 7 volumes contain over 100,000 family notices and include references to over 1 million baptisms, marriages, and burials. It was a monumental work at that time and stands in testimony to the tremendous dedication and effort of Reverend Tanguay.

Numerous errors and omissions have since been discovered and a supplemental volume called **Complément au Dictionnaire Généalogique** was authored by J. Arthur Leboeuf. Proper research of the Tanguay must include a review of the Leboeuf volume.

The more recently published Jetté Dictionary is a more complete work and it will be to your advantage to use it as your primary resource for the years from the start of the French Régime in Canada to about 1730.

HOW DO YOU USE IT ?

The following is an example of the format of the family notices you will find in the Tanguay.

1680, (23 octobre) Québec[5]

III.—COUILLARD, Louis   [Louis II]
    s 15 mai 1728, à St-Pierre-du-Sud.
    1° Vaudry, Marie   [Charles I]
    Louis, b 6 mars 1686, au Cap-St-Ignace[3]; s[3]
13 avril 1686.—*Marie-Anne,* b 1681; s[5] 2 mai 1689.

Figure 1-1

The notices always start with the date of marriage (if known) , the year in bold print and the month and date in parentheses afterwards. Next follows the place of marriage, usually followed by a superscripted number, a "5" in the above example. These superscripted numbers which follow place names and which are later found after the letters "b", "m", and "s" represent the place where the baptisms, marriages, and burials took place or were registered. In this manner, frequent repetition of the same place name is avoided. If a given place name is to be referred to later in the notice the first mention of it will show the superscript number. If the place name will not be referred to again it will not have a superscript number.

In the example above notice that the first mention of "Québec" in the marriage date line is followed by the superscript "5". Later you find this superscript "5" next to the "s" after the child *Marie Anne*'s name. This means that she was buried in the same city referred to above - Québec.

The next line of the notice begins with the Roman numeral III. This refers to the number of the generations that this individual is removed from France. That is:

Number	Degree of Descent or Generations Away from France
I	Immigrant Ancestor - First Generation in New France (Canada)
II	Second Generation in New France
III	Third Generation etc.

Figure 1-2

```
1680, (23 octobre) Quebec⁵

III.—COUILLARD, Louis          [Louis II ]
    s 15 mai 1728, à St-Pierre-du-Sud.
    1° Vaudry, Marie          [Charles I ]
    Louis,  b 6 mars 1686, au Cap-St-Ignace³; s³
13 avril 1686.—Marie-Anne, b 1681; s⁵ 2 mai 1689.
```

Figure 1-1

Now let's continue with our example. It is repeated above and on the next page to facilitate the use of this guide.

The "**III**" that is shown before this individual's name indicates that he is the 3rd generation of his family in New France.

Next comes the last name "COUILLARD" in large capital letters, followed by the first name "Louis" in small capitals.

At the end of the line, in [brackets] is the name of this individual's father, in small capital letters, and his generation or the order of his descent from the immigrant ancestor — [Louis II] . In this case, the father's name is also Louis, and he is the 2nd generation of his family in New France. Other information shown in this example is explained below.

The date and place of his burial.

```
s 15 mai 1728, a St-Pierre-du-Sud
```

Figure 1-3

This is translated "buried on 15 May 1728 at St-Pierre-du-Sud."

The name of his first wife, and the name and degree of descent or generation of her father.

```
1° Vaudry, Marie          [ Charles I ]
```

Figure 1-4

This, "I",means that her father, Charles Vaudry was the immigrant ancestor, or colonist. Additional information about Marie can be found in the family notice under her father's name — Charles Vaudry.

```
1680, (23 octobre) Québec⁵

III.—COUILLARD, Louis                [Louis II ]
      s 15 mai 1728, à St-Pierre-du-Sud.
   1° Vaudry, Marie                  [Charles I ]
      Louis, b 6 mars 1686, au Cap-St-Ignace³; s³
13 avril 1686.—Marie-Anne, b 1681; s⁵ 2 mai 1689.
```

Figure 1-1

The last two lines include the names of their children, in italics; the dates of their baptisms, marriages, and burials; and the names of the parishes where each event was registered.

```
Louis, b 6 mars 1686, au Cap-St-Ignace³; s³
13 avril 1686.—Marie-Anne, b 1681; s⁵ 2 mai 1689.
```

Figure 1-5

Figure 1-5 is translated:

   "*Louis,* baptized on 6 March 1686, at Cap-St-Ignace; buried at the same place on 13 April 1686."

Take particular notice that "Cap-St-Ignace" is followed immediately by a superscripted "3", and the abbreviation for burial, "s", is followed by the same number. This is a good example of the method used by Tanguay to eliminate the need to repeat the names of the parishes or localities.

This is followed by information for the next child in this family.

   "*Marie Anne,* baptized in 1681, buried in Québec on 2 May 1689".

How do we know that she was buried in Québec? Because the abbreviation for burial "s" (for "sépulture") is immediately followed by the superscript "5", and if you look at the example at the top of the page, the first line shows the place of marriage to be "Québec" and it is immediately followed by a superscript "5".

This completes the explanation for the family notice for the first marriage of Louis Couillard.

The date of the first marriage of the individual is always shown in bold-face type. The dates of additional marriages are shown in regular type. This bold-face type then serves to separate the families of the same name. The following is an example of one of the additional marriages of Louis Couillard.

1688, (4 mai) Québec.[5]

2° FORTIN, Marie   [FRANCOIS I]

Geneviève, b 18 juillet 1689. — *Elizabeth*, b 17 avril 1691, a St. Thomas.[8] — *Louise*, b[8] 16 nov. 1692; s[8] 22 nov. 1693. — *Louis*, b[8] 6 fev. 1694; m[8] 17 nov. 1721, à Marthe COTÉ— *Claire-Françoise*, b[8] 7 dec. 1695, hospitaliere dite St. Louis; s[5] 8 mars 1721. — *Marie-Simone*, b[8] 28 mai 1697. — *François*, b[8] 24 nov.1699; m 22 nov. 1728, à Madeleine BERNIER, au Cap St. Ignace. — Joseph, b[8] 18 sept. 1701. — *Jean-Baptiste-Charles*, b[8] 14 juillet 1703; m[8] 19 juin 1729, à Geneviève LANGLOIS. — *Catherine*, b[8] 5 avril 1705; s 7 mai 1706. — *Paul*, b[8] 8 sept. 1707; m 10 nov. 1732, à Marie-Joseph COUTURE, à St-Etienne-de-Beaumont.

Figure 1-6

This example includes the date and place of marriage on the first line.

1688, (4 mai) Québec.[5]

Figure 1-7

This is translated: Married 4 May 1688 at Québec.

Next is the name of the second wife, Marie Fortin, and her father, François, and his degree of descent or generation shown by the Roman numeral " I".

2° FORTIN, Marie,   [FRANÇOIS I]

Figure 1-8

In this case, he is the immigrant ancestor . More information about the wife, Marie, might be found under the family notice for her father, François Fortin. The "2°" indicates that this is the second marriage of Louis Couillard.

The remainder of this family notice is taken up with a listing of the children from this marriage — all 10 of them! The listing includes references to their baptisms, marriages, and burials — when that information is known. In order to facilitate your understanding, a side-by-side translation follows.

FRENCH	ENGLISH
1688, (4 mai) Québec.[5]	married 4 May 1688 at Québec.
2° FORTIN, Marie [FRANÇOIS I]	2nd marriage to Marie Fortin, daughter of François Fortin, the 1st generation in New France.
— *Geneviève*, b 18 juillet 1689.	*Geneviève*, baptized 18 July 1689.
— *Elizabeth*,b 17 avril 1691, a St. Thomas.[8]	*Elizabeth*, baptized 17 April 1691 at St-Thomas.
— *Louise*, b[8] 16 nov. 1692; s[8] 22 nov. 1693.	*Louise*, baptized 16 November 1692 at St-Thomas; buried there on 22 November 1693.
— *Louis*, b[8] 6 fev. 1694; m[8] 17 nov. 1721, à Marthe CÔTÉ.	*Louis*, baptized 6 February 1694 at St-Thomas; married there on 17 November 1721 to Marthe CÔTÉ.
— *Claire-Françoise*, b[8] 7 dec. 1695, hospitaliere dite St. Louis; s[5] 8 mars 1721.	*Claire Françoise*, baptized 7 December 1695 at St-Thomas; Sister of Charity of St-Louis; buried in Québec on 8 March 1721.
— *Marie-Simone*, b[8] 28 mai 1697.	*Marie Simone*, baptized 28 May 1697 at St-Thomas.
— *François*, b[8] 24 nov.1699; m 22 nov. 1728, à Madeleine BERNIER, au Cap-St-Ignace.	*François*, baptized 24 November 1699 at St-Thomas; married at Cap-St-Ignace on 22 November 1728 to Madeleine BERNIER.
—*Joseph*, b[8] 18 sept. 1701.	*Joseph*, baptized 18 September 1701 at St-Thomas.
— *Jean-Baptiste-Charles*, b[8] 14 juillet 1703; m[8] 19 juin 1729, a Geneviève LANGLOIS.	*Jean Baptiste Charles*, baptized 14 July 1703 at St-Thomas; married there on 19 june 1729 to Geneviève LANGLOIS.
— *Catherine*, b[8] 5 avril 1705; s 7 mai 1706.	*Catherine*, baptized on 5 April 1705 at St-Thomas; buried 7 May 1706.
— *Paul*, b[8] 8 sept. 1707; m 10 nov. 1732, à Marie-Joseph COUTURE, à St-Etienne-de-Beaumont.	*Paul*, baptized 8 September 1707 at St-Thomas; married at St-Etienne-de-Beaumont on 10 November 1732 to Marie Joseph COUTURE.
Figure 1-10	Figure 1-11

"Dit" Names

Those of you who have done French-Canadian research will be familiar with this almost uniquely French Canadian custom, the origin of which is not always agreed upon by genealogists. "Dit" literally means "called". For our purposes, it means "also known as", or "sometimes called" or "alias", or "also called". It was used to distinguish individuals having the same surname from one another and it became a very common practice in New France. Consider that the use of surnames as an identifier was only two hundred years old at this time in history and the choice was limited enough that many individuals had common surnames (we still do !). To distinguish one from the other, a second surname was sometimes added. It was usually, but certainly not always, derived in one of several ways including — (1) geographically (where the person came from), (2) a physical attribute of that person, and (3) the individual's occupation. The word "dit" serves to connect the two names, and thus the second name is now commonly referred to as the "dit" name.

Examples include:

GEOGRAPHIC ORIGIN	PERSONAL ATTRIBUTES	PROFESSIONS
Martin Henne dit Portugais (Portuguese)	Jean Romain dit Sanscrainte (without fear)	Maurice Lepine dit Lamusique (the musician)
Jacob Wolfe dit Polonaise (Polish)	Antoine Leblanc dit Jolicoeur (happy hearted)	Joseph Lefèbvre dit Boulanger (the baker)
Charles Faucher dit St. Maurice (from St. Maurice)	Michel Hervé dit Lepetit (small or short)	Jean Louis Larose dit Metivier (the house builder)
Pierre Richard dit Lavallee (from the valley)	François Bigras dit Fauvel (the talker)	Jacques Labonté dit Couturier (the clothier)

Figure 1-12

See also:

Tanguay, Volume 7, pp. 495 - 601.

Stuart, Donna Valley, "French Names in Detroit", Detroit Society For Genealogical Research Magazine, Number 44, (Spring 1981), pp. 131-137.

Laforest, Thomas J., Our French Canadian Ancestors. Lisi Press. Name variations begin in Volume IV.

Quintin, Robert J., The Dit Name: French-Canadian Surnames -Aliases, Adulterations....,162 pp. Quintin Publications

When the baptism, marriage, or burial certificates have been registered under the family name (surname), and under the "dit name", the family notice will generally be in alphabetical order under the family name.

Example:
In a marriage certificate, it might be stated that Jacob Wolfe dit Polonaise, gave his daughter, Marie Louise Wolfe, in marriage. Later on, in the baptismal certificates of her children, she is referred to as Marie Louise Loupe (Wolf), or Marie Louis Polonaise (from Poland). In Tanguay, the names Loupe and Polonaise are referred back to the name Wolfe.

Sometimes it happens that the baptismal certificate of a child is registered under the baptismal name of his father: Louis Raymond, son of Jean Raymond dit Fogas. In Tanguay, the name Raymond is referred back to the name Fogas.

Often, at baptism, the name of a child is registered under the family name of the father, (Hubou) and that same child gets married under the dit name of his father, (Deslongchamps). In this case the marriage certificate states Deslongchamps, but it is still necessary to refer to the name Hubou for other certificates in his family.

Sometimes you will find baptisms in the same family performed on the same day or with an interval of only a few months between. These entries might seem to be errors but they are usually not. The reason for this is that most families waited for the missionary to arrive to baptize their children. But visits from the missionaries to the scattered population centers of New France were sometimes few and far between, and so children were very often baptized many months after their birth.

A few of the family names in the first volume make reference to "dit" names which are only found in volumes 2 to 7. This was done in order to let the researcher know to look in the later volumes for variations.

Notes

THE DROUIN

THE DROUIN

DICTIONNAIRE NATIONAL

DES

CANADIENS FRANÇAIS

(1608-1760)

INSTITUTE GÉNÉALOGIQUE DROUIN
MONTRÉAL, CANADA

NATIONAL DICTIONARY

OF THE

FRENCH CANADIANS

(1608-1760)

DROUIN GENEALOGICAL INSTITUTE
MONTRÉAL, CANADA

What is the Drouin?

The proper title of this resource is Dictionnaire National des Canadiens Français (1680-1760) or National Dictionary of French Canadians (1608-1760). It is called the Drouin after the name of the author. It is the result of over 50 years of researching in the archives and libraries of Europe and North America. It required the microfilming of millions of records as documentation. The work itself is composed of 3 volumes - two volumes of marriage records in alphabetical order and a third volume that contains historical notices, coats of arms, and copies of the signatures of various ancestors. It is in French.

How Do You Use It?

The Drouin is as easy to use as your Webster's Dictionary since it is presented in alphabetical order. The following example is taken from the top of page 18 of Volume 1:

| ARCHAMBAULT | gervais | | touin m. charlotte | pte-aux-tremb. |
| | jn-lefevbre cécile | | germain-baudoin mad. | 6 fév.   1742 |

Figure 2-1

Each marriage in Drouin is given two (2) lines. The first line includes the names of the husband and the wife. On the second line are the names of the parents of the husband and the parents of the wife. To the right of the names is the place and date of the marriage. Subsequent lines, if any, show parish of origin or residence.

Note: In the earliest edition all words are in lower case letters except for the alphabetical listing of the surnames. Many of the first names, place names, and months are abbreviated. In later editions, many of the proper names are capitalized.

Figure 2-1 is interpreted to mean that Gervais Archambault, son of Jean Archambault and Cécile Lefebvre married Marie Charlotte Touin, daughter of Germain Touin and Madeleine Baudoin at Pointe-aux-Trembles on February 6, 1742.

Note in the example that the surnames of the fathers of the bride and groom are not repeated. Only their first names are shown.

A few lines lower on page 18 you can find, again in alphabetical order, the entry for the father and mother of Gervais Archambault.

| ARCHAMBAULT | jean | | lefebvre cécile | montréal |
| | laurent-marchand cath. | | jn.bap-gervaise cunégonde | 4 jun. 1780 |

Figure 2-2

Figure 2-2 is interpreted to mean that Jean Archambault, son of Laurent Archambault and Catherine Marchand, was married in Montreal on 4 June 1708 to Cécile Lefebvre, daughter of Jean Baptiste Lefebvre and Cunégonde Gervaise.

Continue back another generation and you will find, still on page 18 and still in alphabetical order the entry for the parents of Jean Archambault.

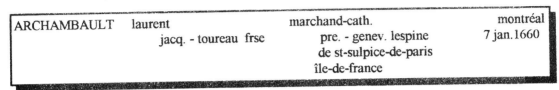

ARCHAMBAULT	laurent	marchand-cath.	montréal
	jacq. - toureau frse	pre. - genev. lespine	7 jan.1660
		de st-sulpice-de-paris	
		île-de-france	

Figure 2-3

Figure 2-3 is translated : Laurent Archambault, son of Jacques Archambault and Françoise Toureau, married in Montréal on 7 January 1660 to Catherine Marchand, daughter of Pierre Marchand and Geneviève Lespine of St-Sulpice parish, Paris, province of Ile-de-France.

This Archambault line continues at the top of page 19 with the following entry for the parents of Laurent Archambault. This is the last entry of this line.

ARCHAMBAULT	jacques	toureau frse.	france
	ant.-renée ouvrard	de france	1629
voir hist	de dompierre dioc. de la		
archambault	rochelle, aunis		
lozeau			

Figure 2-4

Figure 2-4 is translated: Jacques Archambault, son of Antoine Archambault and Renée Ouvrard, of the parish of Dompierre, diocese of La Rochelle, province of Aunis, married Françoise Toureau in France in 1629.

Note that Jacques' parents, Antoine Archambault and Renée Ouvrard, are from Dompierre, diocese of La Rochelle, province of Aunis. This is on the 3rd and 4th lines below their names - "de dompierre dioc. de la rochelle aunis". The wife - Françoise Toureau- has no parents listed. The example shows only "de france" or "from France".

The marginal notation "voir hist. (see history) Archambault and Lozeau" means that those two histories can be found, in alphabetical order, in the historical section, of volume 3.

The words "Vôtre ancêtre", ("Your ancestor") and "Vôtre parent" ("Your relative"), which are included in many of these histories, apply only to a person who is really a relative or descendant.

Referring back to our first two examples, the parents of Marie-Charlotte Touin (Gervais Archambault's wife) and the parents of Cécile Lefebvre (Jean Archambault's wife) can be found, in alphabetical order on page 1289 for Touin and Page 807 for Lefebvre.

Below and on the following 2 pages are listings of the common abbreviations found in Drouin. The blank lines are for your convenience in recording other abbreviations.

Drouin Abbreviations	
voir hist.	see history section (Volume 3)
anc. dir.	direct ancestor of
cont.	marriage contract before a notary

Figure 2-5

Drouin Abbreviations

Masculine First Names and Abbreviations			
Ab.	Abraham	Jacq.	Jacques
Alex.	Alexandre	Jn-Bte.	Jean-Baptiste
Ant.	Antoine	Jn.	Jean
Aug.	Augustin	Jos.	Joseph
Barth.	Barthelémy	Ls.	Louis
Benj.	Benjamin	Nap.	Napoléon
Chs.	Charles	Naz.	Nazaire
Dom.	Dominique	Nic.	Nicolas
Ed.	Edouard	Ph.	Philippe
Etne.	Etienne	Pre.	Pierre
Frs.	François	Ser.	Séraphin
Gab.	Gabriel	Ths.	Thomas
Geo.	Georges	Wm.	William
Guil.	Guillaume	Zeph.	Zéphirin
Ir.	Irenée		

Figure 2-6

Drouin Abbreviations continued

	Feminine First Names and Abbreviations		
Alph.	Alphonsine	Geo.	Georgiana
Am.	Amanda	Germ.	Germaine
Ang.	Angélique	Gert.	Gertrude
Ant.	Antoinette	Henr.	Henriette
Arth.	Arthémise	Jne.	Jeanne
Bern.	Bernadette	Jos.	Josephte
Car.	Caroline	Leoc.	Léocadie
Cath.	Catherine	Lse.	Louise
Cel.	Célanire	Mad.	Madeleine
Charl.	Charlotte	Marc.	Marcelline
Dom.	Domithilde	Marg.	Marguerite
Elis.	Elisabeth	M.	Marie
Eliz.	Elizabeth	Math.	Mathilde
Eug.	Eugénie	Nic.	Nicole
Euph.	Euphrosine	Sch.	Scholastique
Fel.	Félicité	Suz.	Suzanne
Frse.	Françoise	Ther.	Thérèse
Gen.	Geneviève		

Figure 2-7

THE JETTÉ

THE JETTE

Dictionnaire généalogique des familles du Québec
des origines a 1730

René Jetté

avec la collaboration du
Programme de recherche en démographie historique
de l'Université de Montréal

Les Presses de L'Université de Montréal
1983

Genealogical Dictionary of the Families of Québec
from
their Origin to 1730

by René Jetté

in collaboration with the
Demographic History Research Program
of the University of Montreal

University of Montréal Press
1983

What is the Jetté ?

The Jetté is a genealogical dictionary that gives information (pre-1731) about French Canadian families. It was compiled mainly from Catholic parish records of baptisms, marriages, and burials kept by the clergy. The information that is the subject of these records was microfilmed by the Mormon Church in 1977, and the Church provided microfimed copies to the University of Montréal. Thanks to René Jetté and the *Programme de Reserche en Demographie Historique de l'Université de Montréal* (PRDH), all the records were collected, compared, and corrected. In this manner numerous errors made by Tanguay have been eliminated.

The records, once corrected, were entered into a computer database. No parish record was overlooked, all the sources are clearly indicated, distinctions are made between births and baptisms, deaths and burials, all illegitimate children are identified, and isolated individuals are not omitted. The work is exacting, competent, and precise.

Information is included from the beginning of the French Régime in North America from about 1621 to 1730.

The information is provided in either of two different forms. It will be in the form of an **Individual Notice** or a **Family Notice**.

The **Individual Notice** provides genealogical information about one individual only.

The **Family Notice** provides genealogical information about a family — husband, wife, and children. Most of the notices are family notices.

The individual notices are shown in **alphabetical** order by the surname of the individual. Family notices are shown in **alphabetical** order by the surname of the husband.

For a given surname, the **individual notices** are shown first, in **alphabetical** order by first name.

The **family notices** follow, in **chronological** order, by the date of the first marriage of the husband.

How Do You Use It?

Since the Jetté is book of genealogies in alphabetical order the most difficult thing about using it is that it is in French. If you do not understand French it can be a chore trying to translate it.

The following information will be important to the understanding of how the genealogies were created and what information they contain.

Four examples shown in the introduction to Jette are included along with an English translation.

Figure 3-1 is an example of a Family Notice with children.
Figure 3-2 is an example of an Individual Notice.
Figure 3-3 is an example of a Family Notice without children.
Figure 3-4 is an additional example of a Family Notice with children.

These examples will be referred to often in the explanation that follows. The reader should attempt to follow along to facilitate understanding.

A listing of commonly used abbreviations, symbols, and terms is also included for the researcher's convenience.

Before we begin it will be helpful to know a few basics, such as:

The dates are shown in the following order (DD-MM-YYYY), where D=Day, M=Month, and Y=Year. For example, 07-06-1732 means 7 June 1732; 30-01-1694 means 30 January 1694; 02-08-1836 means 02 August 1836.

The other most basic thing to know is that most of the records were kept by the parish churches and they documented events that took place in the church such as baptisms, marriages, and burials. Therefore you will find these records to be the most common. Dates of birth and death were not required and are not always shown. Common abbreviations are b=baptism, m=marriage, s=burial, n=born, and d=died.

Our explanation will continue on the next page with the first part of Figure 3-1 dealing with the husband and wife sections of the Family Notice along with an explanation. Next will follow the listing of the children from Figure 3-1 and following that, an explanation of what is shown.

Family Notice with Children — Figure 3-1

French Version

LABBÉ dit **LACROIX,** Pierre

(François & Marie **FOREST** ou **FOURÉ**)

b 30-06-1643 Nôtre-Dame-des-Marais,

v. La Ferté-Bernard,

ar. Mamers,

év. LeMans, Maine, (Sarthe);

s 04-01-1709 St-François, Î. O. ;

au rec. 81, à l'Île d'Orléans;

arrivé 30-06-1665,

soldat de la compagnie de **MONTEIL**
au régiment de **CARIGNAN.**

[MSGCF (84): 75]

m 31-07-**1672** Ste-Famille, Î. O.
(ct 16-07-1670 Vachon)

BERNARD, Catherine

(veuve Jacques DELAUNAY)

d 23 s 24-10-1672 Ste-Famille, Î. O. (43 ans).

SANS POSTÉRITÉ

m 10-04-**1674** Beaupré
(ct 08 Vachon)

MEUNIER, Marguerite

(Mathurin & Françoise FAFARD)

English Translation

LABBE also called LACROIX, Pierre

(son of François & Marie **FOREST** or **FOURÉ**)

born 30 June 1643 at Nôtre-Dame-des-Marais,

village of La Ferté-Bernard,

district of Mamers,

diocese of Le Mans, Maine, (Sarthe);

buried 04 January 1709 at St-François, Île d'Orleans;

at Île d'Orleans according to the 1681 census;

arrived on 30 June 1665,

was a soldier in the Company of MONTEIL in the Carignan Regiment.

Source: [Mémoires de la Société Généalogique Canadienne- Française, volume 84, page 75]

first marriage 31 July 1672 at Ste-Famille, Île d'Orleans
(marriage contract dated 16 July 1670 before Notary Vachon)

BERNARD, Catherine

(widow of Jacques DELAUNAY)

died 23 buried 24 October 1672 at Ste-Famille, Île d' Orleans (43 years old).

WITHOUT DESCENDANTS

second marriage, 10 April 1674 at Beaupré
(marriage contract dated 08 April 1674 before Notary Vachon)

MEUNIER, Marguerite

(daughter of Mathurin & Françoise FAFARD)

Family notices are described in 3 sections: (1) the husband's information, (2) the wife's information, and (3) the children's information.

The husband's information will include, when known, the following :

His family name, in bold capital letters to facilitate indexing and searching; his "dit" name, where applicable, in bold, italic, small capital letters; and his first name.

LABBÉ dit *LACROIX*, Pierre

See Tanguay 7 for a discussion of the "dit" name.

Next will follow, in parentheses, the first name of his father, and the first and last name of his mother. In French-Canadian research the last name of the father is always assumed to be the same as the last name of the child and so it is usually not shown.

(François & Marie FOREST ou FOURÉ)

If the names of the parents are not known, this will be shown as (...), 3 dots enclosed in parentheses. An example of this can be seen in Figure 3-2, page 10.

If the husband was born in this country (New France), or emigrated (ususally from France) with at least one of his parents, this information will refer you back to the Family Notice of his parents.

If the individual immigrated without his parents, as in this example, those parents will not have their own Family Notice.

If the individual immigrated, and the names of his parents are known, then their names are usually followed by his place of origin, if known.

Next, in order, is the date and place of his birth and baptism.

(Fr) b 30-06-1643 Nôtre-Dame-des-Marias
(Eng) baptized 30 June 1643 at Nôtre-Dame-des-Marias

Note again that the date is in the format (DD-MM-YYYY), where D=Day, M=Month,Y=Year.

The next 3 lines in our example include references to the village, district and diocese where Pierre was baptized.

v. La Ferté-Bernard	(village of La Ferté-Bernard)
ar. Mamers	(district of Mamers)
év. LeMans, Maine, (Sarthe)	(diocese of LeMans, Maine (Sarthe))

Following, is the date and place of his death and burial, if known.

(Fr)	s 04-01-1709 St-François, Î. O.
(Eng)	buried 04 January 1709 at St-François,Île d'Orleans

Additional information about the husband shown below this in our example includes when he arrived, his occupation, and where he was in the 1681 census along with a reference to the source of the information.

The date and place of marriage serves to separate the information of the husband from the information of the wife. Included in this area is a reference to any marriage contract along with the date of the contract and the name of the notary.

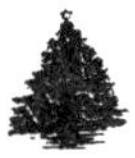

m 31-07-1672 Ste-Famille Î O.
(ct 16-07-1670 Vachon)

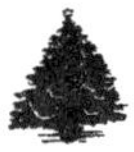

married on 31 July 1672 at Ste-Famille, Ile d'Orleans
(marriage contract signed 16 July 1670 before Notary Vachon)

If a marriage record is not found, then the date and place of the marriage contract is presumed to be the date and place of the marriage.

The tree icons indicate the number of marriages entered into by the husband:

1 tree = first marriage
2 trees = second marriage, etc.

Next follows the wife's information and includes, when known:
Her family name, in bold capital letters, her "dit" name, if one exists, in bold italic capitals, and her first name.

BERNARD, Catherine

Next, the names of her parents, in parentheses, if this is her first marriage. In this case, this is a subsequent marriage and so the parents are not mentioned.

The name of her former spouse, in parentheses, if she is a widow.

(Fr) (veuve Jacques DELAUNAY)   **(Eng)** (widow of Jacques DELAUNAY)

Next will usually follow, the date and place of her birth and baptism, if known. This is not shown in our example.

This will be followed by the date and place of her death and burial, if known.

(Fr)   d 23 s 24-10-1672 Ste-Famille, Î. O.
(Eng)   died 23, buried on 24 October 1672 at Ste-Famille, Île d'Orleans.

In French, the "d" stands for "décès" or died; "s" stands for "sépulture" or burial.

The next item in the example is the statement "SANS POSTERITE". This is translated "Without Descendants", in other words, childless.

Continuing with Figure 3-1, reference to the husband's (Pierre) second marriage is next.

    m 10-04-1674 Beaupré   (married 10 April 1674 at Beaupré)
(ct 08 Vachon)   (Marriage Contract signed 8 October 1674
before Notary Vachon)

This is followed by the name of the second wife.

MEUNIER, Marguerite

Followed by the names of her parents, in parentheses.

(Mathurin & Francoise FAFARD)

This provides a lead to further research on her family.

In closing, mention is made of Marguerite's remarriage in 1710 to Jean Deblois.

rem 1710 Jean DEBLOIS

This page and the following page is a listing of the 13 children born to Pierre LABBE dit LACROIX and his wife, Marguerite MEUNIER. It has been enlarged to facilitate understanding.

French Version	English Translation
1. *Marguerite* n 24-03 b 04-04-1675 Ste-Famille, Île d'Orleans d 13-05-1691 Hôtel-Dieu Québec.	1. *Marguerite*, born 24 Mar, bapt 04 April 1675 Ste-Famille, Île d'Orleans died 13 May 1691 at the Hospital in Québec
2. *Jacques* n 08 b 09-10-1676 Ste-Famille, Île d'Orleans d 07 s 08-11-1676 id.	2. *Jacques*, born 08, baptized 09 October 1676 Ste-Famille, Île d'Orleans died 07 buried 08 November 1676 at the same place.
3. *Marie* n 13 b 15-12-1677 Ste-Famille, Île d'Orleans d 19 s 20 id.	3. *Marie*, born 13 baptized 15 December 1677 Ste-Famille, Île d'Orleans died 19 buried 20 1676 at the same place.
4. *Anne* n 16 b 17-07-1679 St-François, Île d'Orleans m 1694 Jean-François ALLAIRE; m annulé ct 04-03-1694 Chambalon: Jacques MARCEAU	4. *Anne*, born 16 baptized 17 July 1679 St-François, Île d'Orleans married 1694 Jean François ALLAIRE marriage contract to Jacques Marceau annulled, dated 04 March 1694 before Notary Chambalon
5. *François* b 10-09-1681 St-François, Île d'Orleans s 14-08-1688 id.	5. *François*, born 10 September 1681 St-François, Île d'Orleans buried 14 August 1688 at the same place.

French Version	English Translation
6. Anonyme de sexe indéterminé n ond., d et s 22-10-1683 St-François, Île d'Orleans	6. Unnamed child, sex not determined born, baptized at home, died, and buried on 22 October 1683 St-François, Île d'Orleans
7. *Marie* n 15 b 17-03-1685 St-François, Île d'Orleans m 1699 Pierre Boucher.	7. *Marie*, born 15, baptized 17 March 1685 St-François Île d'Orleans married 1699 Pierre Boucher.
8. *Jacques* n 10 b 12-05-1687 St-François, Île d'Orleans m 1709 Françoise Deblois	8. *Jacques,* born 10, baptized 12 May 1687 at St-François, Île d'Orleans married Françoise Deblois in 1709.
9. *Pierre* n et b 28-03-1689 St-François, Île d'Orleans s 07-04-1689 id.	9. *Pierre*, born and baptized 28 March 1689 at St-François, Île d'Orleans buried 07 April 1689 at the same place.
10. *Madeleine* b 28-12-1690 St-François, Île d'Orleans m 1710 Jean-Baptiste Deblois.	10. *Madeleine*, born 28 December 1690 at St-François, Île d'Orleans married 1710 to Jean Baptiste Deblois.
11. *Pierre* n vers 1692, 32 ans en 1720, m 1715 Reine Garinet.	11. *Pierre*, born about 1692, 32 years old in 1720, married in 1715 to Reine Garinet.
12. *Jean* n 19 b 20-04-1699 St-François Île d'Orleans m 1724 Marie Lepage.	12. *Jean,* born 19, baptized 20 April 1699 at St-François, Île d'Orleans married in 1724 to Marie Lepage.
13. *Geneviève* n 17 b 18-02-1701 St-François, Île d'Orleans m 1718 Pierre Martineau.	13. *Geneviève*, born 17, baptized 18 Feb 1701 St-François, Île d'Orleans married in 1718 to Pierre Martineau.

The children of this marriage are listed in the order of their birth.

For each child is listed:

The first name or name bestowed at baptism, in italics.

The "dit" or "also called" name if used by this child.

The date and place of birth and baptism.

The date and place of death and burial, if he died unmarried.

If married, the date and name of his first wife. In this case, the rest of this child's history might be found with his own family notice.

If the child is a girl, the rest of her history might be found with the family notice of her husband.

This same format is followed for each of the husband's remarriages. That is, the date and place of remarriage, the history of the new wife, and a listing of the children of this union.

In conclusion, a family notice contains the history of the husband, from his first marriage to his death, the history of his successive wives from the present marriage to either their remarriage or death, and the history of each of the children from their birth to their marriage or death.

Individual Notices — Figure 3-2

The following is an example of an Individual Notice. It has been enlarged to facilitate understanding, and is explained on the next page.

French Version	English Translation
LABBÉ dit **VILLENEUVE,** Jean	**LABBE** dit **VILLENEUVE,** Jean
(...)	(parents unknown)
de v. et archev. Paris;	of the city and archdiocese of Paris;
d après 06-09-1694, Québec;	died after 09 June 1694 at Québec;
25 ans au rec. 66, à Beaupré,	25 years old in the 1666 census of Beaupré,
domestique engagé de Jean LEPAGE;	engaged in service to Jean LEPAGE;
confirmé 12-03-1666 L'Ange-Gardien;	confirmed on 12 March 1666 at L'Ange-Gardien;
cité 14-05-1686 Québec, meunier de Marie DUPONT	mentioned as being in Québec on 14 May 1686, as a miller for Marie DUPONT;
et 26-08-1687 Charlesbourg, brasseur à la brasserie;	and on 26 August 1687 in Charlesbourg, as a brewer in a brewery;
meunier des Jésuites en 1694;	and as a miller for the Jesuits in 1694;
ENFANT NATUREL	***ILLEGITIMATE CHILD***
(mère: Marie-Anne FAYE, fille de Pierre & Marie CHAUVET):	(mother: Marie Anne FAYE, daughter of Pierre Faye & Marie Chauvet):
Marie-Jeanne n 13 b 14-07-1694 Charlesbourg	*Marie Jeanne,* born 13th, baptized 14 July 1694 at Charlesbourg,
m 1715 Jacques RACICOT.	married 1715 to Jacques RACICOT.

The individual notice is layed out in a format similar to the husband's section in a family notice. Figure 3-2 is an individual notice and it contains the following:

His family name, in bold capital letters to facilitate indexing and searching; his "dit" name, where applicable, in bold, italic, small capital letters; and his first name.

LABBÉ dit *VILLENEUEVE,* Jean

The first name of his father and the first and last name of his mother, in parentheses, or (...) to indicate that the names of the parents are not known, as in this case.

If the individual was born in this country (New France), or emigrated (usually from France) with at least one of his parents, this information will refer you back to the family notice of his parents.

If the individual immigrated without his parents, those parents will not have a notice.

If the individual immigrated and the names of his parents are known then their names are usually followed by his place of origin, if known. In this case, he is from the city and archdiocese of Paris.

(Fr)   *de v. et archev. Paris;*
(Eng)   *of the city and archdiocese of Paris;*

Next in order is the date and place of his birth and baptism. In this case this information was not known.

Next the date and place of his death and burial, when this information in known.

(Fr)   *d après 06-09-1694, Québec*
(Eng)   *died after 9 June 1694 at Québec*

Other information included in this example includes the date of his confirmation, his status in the census of 1666, and his occupations.

Of note in this Individual Notice is the fact that Jean, the subject of this notice, fathered an illegitimate child (ENFANT NATUREL). This child, Marie-Jeanne, was born on 14 July 1694 at Charlesbourg. The mother, Marie-Anne Faye, was the daughter of Pierre and Marie Chauvet.

Special Rules

The general structure of these notices could be subject to modifications, either because the sources consulted did not provide the necessary information, or because they contained even more information that helped provide a more complete history.

If the notice is missing certain information, the following rules apply:

The word "vers" (about) followed by a date is used when the marriage or birth date is not known. Figure   child 11

    (Fr) Pierre n vers 1692   *(Eng)   Pierre born about 1692*

If the marriage date was not known, then it was assumed that the couple married in the year preceding the birth of their first child. The place of marriage, if not known, is also assumed to be the place of the birth of the first child.

If the date of birth was not known, then it was usually calculated from a report of age during a subsequent event, such as a census. Example 3, 11th child.

    (Fr)   *(n vers 1692, 32 ans en 1720)*

    (Eng)   *(born about 1692, 32 years old in 1720)*

Each time the birth or baptismal dates were not known (which is especially true in the case of immigrants) this information was obtained from supplemental information such as lists of ages given at various events (weddings, funerals, censuses, etc.) Example 1.

Three dots, ... , indicate either a name, part of a name, or a date, that could not be obtained through any other source of information.

When the names of the parents or the spouse are not found as the subject of their own family or individual notices, then their place of origin is mentioned, if known, and if outside of Québec.

If the origin of a person who appeared to be an immigrant is not known, then the phrase *("d'origine inconnue") "of unknown origin"* is shown.

If the person appeared to be born in Québec, then his place of residence or origin in Québec will be stated.

The dates of death and burial are frequently missing because the information was not found. In this case, if it was known that the individual died before or after a certain date, that information is noted. Example 2.

(Fr)   *(d après 06-09-1694)*

(Eng)   *(died after 9 June 1694)*

This approximate date is shown in the space provided for the date of death. It is followed by the presumed place of death.

Various consulted sources provided important additional information which was inserted in the notices.

When the names of the parents are shown additional information might include whether they were still living or already deceased at the marriage of their children.

(Fr)   († for feu (masculine) or feue (feminine))

(Eng)   († for deceased).

Their profession is sometimes known.

Their dates of marriage and death are sometimes known.

All of this information is shown between the parentheses that enclose their names.

If information about additional generations of ancestors in France is known then this information is indented at the end of the notice.

These individuals are numbered according to the Stradonitz method. The immigrant husband is 1, his parents are 2 & 3, his paternal grandparents are 4 & 5, his maternal grandparents are 6 & 7 etc.

A large number of notices contain additional pieces of information of a genealogical, historical, or professional nature.

All of this information is placed after the mention of death and always ends, if applicable, with a listing in square brackets [ ] of the sources for this information. Examples 1, 3.

This additional information might include:

Information from censuses - date of the census, age, place of residence, profession.
Examples 2, 3.

The date of arrival . Example 3.

> *(Fr)*   *("arrivé 30-06-1665")*
>
> *(Eng)*   *(arrived on 30 June 1665).*

The date of the first mention of the individual in civil documents. For example, as a witness to a contract, or as a party to a land transaction. This is usually followed by the name of the Notary. Example 1.

> *(Fr)*   *("cité ct. Audouart 24-02-1649, soldat du fort")*
>
> *(Eng)*   *(mentioned as a garrison soldier in a contract*
>   *by Notary Audouart on 24 February 1694) .*

A listing of some of the professions practiced. Examples 1, 2, 3.

The stages of a career (in the clergy, in the army, in the administration) Examples 1, 2, 3.

The date of departure or the date and occasion of last mention.

Any transactions regarding the seigneuries (divisions of land) such as concessions given, purchases, sales, and trades.

Any marriage contracts signed and marriages annulled. Example 3, 4th child .

(Fr)   *(m annulé ct 04-03-1694 Chambalon: Jacques Marceau)*

(Eng)   *(marriage to Jacques Marceau annulled 04 March 1694*
                    in a contract before Notary Chambalon).

The notice of an illegitimate child which includes the name of the child, the name of the father, the name of the natural mother, along with a reference to the parents or spouse of the natural mother. Example 2.

(Fr)   **ENFANT NATUREL**

(Eng)   **Illegitimate child**

Notes

French Version	English Translation
LABAT, dit *FONTARABIE,* Mathieu	**LABAT** dit FONTARABIE, Matthew
(veuf René MONTET)	(widower of René MONTET)
(Jacques & Marie FORTIN)	(daughter of Jacques Montet and Marie Fortin)
de St-Gilles-de-Bourg-sur-Mer	of St-Gilles-de-Bourg-sur-Mer
(or Bourg-sur-Gironde),	(or Bourg-sur-Gironde),
ar. Blaye,	department of Blaye,
archev. Bordeaux,	diocese of Bordeaux,
Gascogne (Gironde);	Gascogne (Gironde);
s 09-12-1654 Trois-Rivières	buried 09 December 1654 at Trois-Rivières
(50 ans)	(50 years old)
(attaqué par les Iroquois 23-11-1654);	(attacked by the Iroquois on 23 November 1654);
cité ct Audouart 24-02-1649, soldat du fort.	mentioned in a contract by Notary Audouart 24 February 1649, as a soldier of the fort.
[MSGCF (100): 85-88]	[Source: Mémoires de la Société Généalogique Canadienne-Française, volume 100, pages 85-88]
m ct 26-01-1653 Ameau (Trois-Rivières)	marriage contract 26 January **1653** before Notary Ameau at Trois-Rivières
DENOT, Marie	DENOT, Marie
(veuve Étienne Vien)	(widow of Étienne VIEN)
rem. 1655 Louis OZANNE.	remarried in 1655 to Louis OZANNE.
SANS POSTÉRITÉ	WITHOUT DESCENDANTS.

Family Notice With Children — Figure 3-4

French Version

LABBÉ, Jacques (Pierre & Marguerite MEUNIER) .

   m 25-11-**1709** Ste-Famille, Î.O.
   (ct 06 Jacob père)

DEBLOIS, Françoise (Jean & Françoise ROUSSEAU).

1. *Françoise* n et b 20-11-1710 St-François, Î.O.

2. *Marie-Madeleine* n et b 12-09-1712 St-Françoise, Î.O.
   d 17 s 18-07-1730 id.

3. *Jacques* n et b 11-09-1714 St-François, Î.O.
   d 01 s 04-10-1714 St-Jean, Î.O.

4. *Charles* n et b 16-12-1715 St-François, Î.O.

5. *Marie-Marthe* n et b 23-12-1720 St-François, Î.O.

6. *Joseph-Marie* n et b 13-03-1720 St-François, Î.O.
   d 13 b 14 id.

7. *Jacques* n et b 10-05-1721 St-François, Î.O.

8. *Pierre* n 17 b 18-08-1723 St-François, Î.O.

9. *Joseph* n 26 b 27-09-1725 St-Jean, Î.O.

10. *Jean-Baptiste* n 10 b 11-09-1727 St-François, Î.O.

11. *François* n 07 b 08-01-1730 St-François, Î.O.
   d et s 15-07-1730 id.

English Translation

Labbé, Jacques, son of Pierre Labbé and Marguerite Meunier.

Married 25 November 1709 at Ste-Famille, Île d'Orleans (marriage contract dated 06 November 1709 before Notary Jacob)

to Françoise Deblois, daughter of Jean Deblois and Françoise Rousseau.

1. *Françoise*, born and baptized on 20 November 1710 at St-François, Île d'Orleans.

2. *Marie Madeleine,* born and baptized on 12 September 1712 at St-François, Île d'Orleans; died 17 July, 1730, buried on the 18th of July at the same place.

3. *Jacques,* born and baptized on 11 September 1714 at St-François, Ile d'Orleans. Died on 01 October, 1714 and buried on 04 October at St-Jean, Île d'Orleans.

4. *Charles,* born and baptized on 16 December 1715 at St-François, Île d'Orleans

5. *Marie Marthe*, born and baptized on 23 December 1720 at St-François, Île d'Orleans;

6. *Joseph Marie*, born and baptized on 13 March 1720 at St-François, Île d'Orleans. Died on the 13th of December, and was buried on the 14th of December at this same place.

7. *Jacques*, born and baptized on 10 May 1721 at St-François, Île d'Orleans,

8. *Pierre*, born on 17 August 1723, and baptized on the 18th of August at St-François, Île d'Orleans.

9. *Joseph*, born 26 September 1725, baptized on 27 September at St-Jean, Île d'Orleans.

10. *Jean Baptiste*, born 10 September 1727, baptized on 11 September at St-François, Île d'Orleans.

11. *Francois*, born 07 January 1730, baptized on the 8th at St-François, Île d'Orleans. Died and was buried on 15 July 1730 at the same place.

Abbreviations and Definitions, French to English — Figure 3-5

French Abbreviations and Symbols	French Definition	English Definition
ar.	arrondissement	district
archev.	archevêché	archdiocese
b	baptême	baptism
cité	cité	mentioned in
C.N.D.	Congrégation-Notre-Dame	Congregation of Notre Dame (order of Roman Catholic nuns)
confirmé	confirmé	confirmed
ct	contrat	contract
d	décès	death
év.	évêché	diocese
fille, fils		daughter, son
id.	au même endroit	of the same place
m	mariage	marriage
mère		mother
n	naissance	birth
père		father
rec.	recensement	census
rem.	remariage	remarriage
s	sépulture	burial
sans postérité		without descendants
v.	ville	town/city
vers		about
veuf, veuve		widow, widower
&	et	and
...	renseignement non disponible	information not available
(...)	nom des parents inconnus	name of parents unknown
†	feu, feue	deceased male, deceased female
1 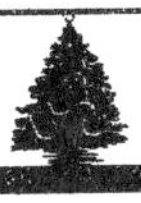 2 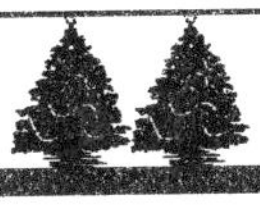	ordre de mariage, 1er, 2e etc.	order of marriage, 1st, 2nd etc.

THE PRDH

The PRDH

Répertoire des Actes de Baptême, Mariage, Sépulture et des Recensements du Québec Ancien

Repertory of the Acts of Baptism, Marriage, Burial and Censuses of Old Québec

Created by the
Programme de Recherche en Démographie Historique
or PRDH,
(Research Program in Historical Demography)
at the University of Montréal

Published under the direction of
Hebert Charbonneau and Jacques Legare

Les Presses de L'université de Montréal
Montréal, Canada
1980

What is the PRDH ?

PRDH stands for Programme de Recherche en Demographic Historique. In English it is called the Research Program in Historical Demography. The primary objective of this program at the University of Montreal was to read and transcribe all of the parish records of Ancient Quebec. As the work progressed other records were added: censuses, confirmations, recantations, ship's lists, hospital sick lists, and notary records of marriage contracts.

The information transcribed was computerized to facilitate its use and eventual publication.

This massive undertaking, which eventually led to the publication of the 47 volumes, now known as the PRDH, began in 1966.

Information gathered from these records included the full names of almost **everyone** listed on a baptismal, marriage, or burial certificate, including witnesses and spouses. It also included, for **every** individual mentioned, their sex, age, marital status, whether living or deceased, occupation, kinship, and places of residence and origin if that information was available.

It covers the period from the beginning of old Quebec to 1765. This covers the entire period of the French Regime.

It is probably the most complete documentation of these records that will ever be published.

NOTES:

Introduction

The repertory series or PRDH is composed of 47 volumes. The primary sources for the information contained in those volumes are parish records of baptisms, marriages, burials, confirmations, recantations, and confirmations. The series also contains notarial records of marriages; civil census records; hospital sick lists; and some ship's passenger lists.

The volumes are divided into five distinct periods of time:

Volumes	Period(s)
1 to 7	to 1699
8 to 17	1700 - 1729
18 to 30	1730 - 1749
31 to 45	1750 - 1765
46 to 47	1700 - 1765

Figure 4-1

Type Codes

We mentioned that the volumes were comprised of many different types of records. To facilitate your research, each type of record has been given a distinct code. These codes are:

Code	Type	Code	Type
A	Recantation	M	Marriage
B	Baptism	N	Marriage Contract
C	Confirmation	R	Census
H	Hospital Sick List	S	Burial
L	List of Migrants	Z	Marriage Annulment

Figure 4-2

Source Codes

We previously mentioned that the PRDH was made up of records from many different sources. The primary sources are from parish records. To facilitate researching the records, each source of document has been given a 3 digit code. This 3 digit code represents the source or place of origin of the document. A listing of these can be found in Appendix 2, Contents of the Repertoires by Source. If the source is a parish, as most of them are, then you can expect to find codes such as:

Source	Code
St-François-du-Lac	631
St-Joseph	041
Ste-Geneviève	235
Hôpital-Général-de-Montréal	392

Figure 4-3

If someone asked you —

What does "B 631", or "S 392", or "M 041", mean to you?

You should be able to tell them —

The first one is a reference to a baptism (B) in the parish of St- Francois-du-Lac (631).

The second is a reference to a burial (S) from the Hôpital-Général-de-Montréal (General Hospital of Montreal) (392).

The third is a reference to a marriage (M) in the parish of St-Joseph (041).

The Index (Indices)

Probably the easiest way to start your research is to look in the index. The PRDH contains several volumes of indices. They are:

Volume	Contents	Period
7	Index to Volumes 1-6	to 1699
16	Index to Volumes 8-15 (A-G)	1700-1729
17	Index to Volumes 8-15 (H-Z)	1700-1729
29	Index to Volumes 18-28 (A-G)	1730-1749
30	Index to Volumes 18-28 (H-Z)	1730-1749
43	Index to Volumes 31-42 (A-D)	1750-1765
44	Index to Volumes 31-42 (E-L)	1750-1765
45	Index to Volumes 31-42 (M-Z)	1750-1765
47	Index to Volumes 46-47	1700-1765

Figure 4-4

In addition, starting with Volume 8, each volume contains an index by parish that is found right after the parish records. But for now we won't worry about that. Let's just concentrate on the main index (indices).

The general index includes the following information in this format:

Figure 4-5

M 451 1720-11-11 1 01 6
Document Code
Source Code
Date of Document
Sequence #
Referral #
Volume #

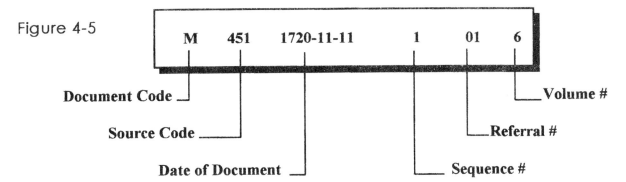

We've already covered the Document Code and the Source Code, and have a good understanding of what the date of the document is. The other items shown above are:

Volume

This refers to the number of the Volume that the information will be found in.

Referral

This is the order that your ancestor is referred to in the document. Whether he was the 1st, 2nd, or the 3rd person listed in the document. For example, in a baptismal document, the person being baptized should be "01". In a marriage document, the groom and bride should be "01" and "02". The remaining individuals at the ceremony will be listed as mentioned in the document. The father and mother of the groom would probably be "03" and "04". The father and mother of the bride, "05" and "06", etc.. So when researching, if you are looking for a baptism, and you find the name you are looking for and it shows Referral #06, then you can be sure that this is not the record you are looking for because this person is just a witness or godparent in that baptism.

Sequence

When two or more documents of the same type were recorded in the same parish on the same day, the date in the index is followed by a sequence number. The first document is zero (0), and the following documents are numbered "1", "2", "3", etc.

BRANCHAULT

CHARLES	B	271	1695-03-01	01	5
	B	271	1695-03-01	02	5
	S	271	1695-03-05	01	5
	S	271	1695-03-05	02	5
	B	271	1696-05-01	02	5
JACQUES	B	271	1696-05-01	01	5

Figure 4-6

BRANCHEREAU

CHARLES	N	NOT	1694-01-10		01	6
	M	385	1694-02-22	#1	01	2
JACQUES	M	385	1694-02-22	#1	03	2

Figure 4-7

The first listing for **Charles Branchault** is in a baptismal record *(B)*, in the parish of Laprairie *(271)*, on *March 1, 1695*. In this document, Charles is the first person referred to *(01)*, and this information can be found in Volume *5*.

The second listing for **Charles Branchault** is in a baptismal record *(B)*, in the parish of Laprairie *(271)*, on *March 1, 1695*. In this document, Charles is the second person referred to *(02)*, and this information can be found in Volume *5*. This number indicates that he is the father of the Charles cited above.

The third listing for **Charles Branchault** is in a burial record *(S)*, in the parish of Laprairie *(271)*, on *March 5, 1695*. In this document, Charles is the first person referred to *(01)*, and this information can be found in Volume *5*.

The first listing for **Charles Branchereau** is a marriage contract *(N)*, in the notary records *(NOT)*, on *January 10, 1694*. In this document, Charles is the first person referred to (01), and this information can be found in Volume *6*.

The second listing for **Charles Branchereau** is in a marriage record *(M)*, in the parish of St. Laurent, Ile-d'Orléans *(385)* on *February 22, 1694*. This is the second marriage document listed in this parish on this date (*#1*), Charles is the first person referred to *(01)*, and the information can be found in Volume *2*.

After the Index

Once you obtain the citation from the index, **write it down**. The next step is to find that listing in the volumes. Since most of the documents are listed by parish in chronological order by baptisms, marriages, or burials, they must be researched that way.

First, find the...Volume.

Then, in that volume, find the..Parish.

Then look for the section for....................Baptisms............B.

                                        Marriages..........M.

                                        Burials...............S.

Then look for your ....Date.

Remember, the documents are in chronological order!

The Top of the Page

The top line of each page indicates the type of records shown (left side), the name of the parish the records are from (center), and the type code and source code of those records (right side). This is illustrated in Figures 4-8, 4-9, and 4-10 below.

| BAPTEMES | LA-NATIVITE-DE-LA-B.V.M.-DE-LAPRAIRIE | B 271 |

Figure 4-8

| CONTRATS DE MARIAGE | | N NOT |

Figure 4-9

| RESCENSEMENT DE 1760 | ST-ANTOINE-DE-LA-RIVIERE-DU-LOUP | R 331 |

Figure 4-10

Document - General Information

Figure 4-11

	B 1695-03-02		N 1695-03-01			
01	**CHARLES/BRANCHAULT**				C	M
02	CHARLES/BRANCHAULT	P:90	PERE		M	M
03	MARTHE/GARAND		MERE		M	F
04	/DENOYAN	P:03				M
05	ROBERT/GROTON	P:08				M
06	MARIE/RIVET		r:C.P.			F
07	L/GEOFFROY	P:02	r:C.P.		C	M

The main part of the document is always written in the same order: the referral number and the list of names is given, on the left, in the following order:

- The primary individual
- The parents or spouse
- Other persons, in their order of appearance in the certificate
- The author of the document is always last

To the right of the document is shown:

⇒ The relationship between the individuals, if known. Father, mother, sister, brother, etc.

⇒ The marital status:
- C.............Single   M.............Married
- V.............Widowed   S.............Separated

⇒ Presence.   If the individual was not present, it will probably show:
- D.............Deceased

⇒ The sex of the person listed, if known.
- M..............Male
- F................Female
- I.................Unknown

⇒ All other information appears in the center of the document, usually on the same line or on an additional line, if needed. The codes are:
- H................Number of days of hospitalization
- O...............Place of origin, infull, followed by the code
- P................Code for occupation
- R................Place of residence, in full, followed by the code.
- S................Mention of whether the document was signed, followed by "oui" (yes) or "non" (no).

Document - Baptism

Figure 4-12

	B 1695-03-02	N	1695-03-01		
01	**CHARLES/BRANCHAULT**			C	M
02	CHARLES/BRANCHAULT	P:90	PERE	M	M
03	MARTHE/GARAND		MERE	M	F
04	/DENOYAN	P:03			M
05	ROBERT/GROTON	P:08			M
06	MARIE/RIVET		r:C.P.		F
07	L/GEOFFROY	P:02	r:C.P.	C	M

The top line of the document indicates the date of the baptism, (B   1695-03-02), followed by the date of the birth (N   1695-03-01).

There were seven (7) people mentioned in the baptismal record. This is shown on the left side of the document (01 to 07).

01. **Charles Branchault.** His number and name in bold print means that he is the primary subject of this event. He is single (C). He is male (M).

02. **Charles Branchault.** He is the father (PERE). He is married (M). He is male (M). His profession is soldier (P:90).

03. **Marthe Garand.** She is the mother (MERE). She is married (M). She is female (F).

04. **Mr. Denoyon.** First name not mentioned. He is male (M). His profession is army officer (P:03). He is a witness, and could possibly be the godfather.

05. **Robert Groton.** His profession is non-commissioned officer (P:08). He is male (M). He is a witness and could be the godfather.

06. **Marie Rivet.** She resides in this parish (R:C.P.) She is female (F). She could be the godmother.

07. **L. Geoffroy.** He is the priest (P:02). He resides in this parish (R:C.P.). He is single (C). He is male.

Document - Marriage

01	CHARLES/BRANCHEREAU	28 ANS	o:FRANCE,OUEST, RURAL (872)		C		M
02	ANNE/FAY		r:QUÉBEC (451)		C		F
03	JACQUES/BRONCHEREAU	*PERE DE 01* p:51	r: FRANCE, OUEST, RURAL (872)				M
04	ANTOINETTE/VINCENT	*MERE DE 01*	r: FRANCE,OUEST, RURAL (872)		M	D	F
05	PIERRE/FAYE	*PERE DE 02*	r: QUÉBEC (451)		M	D	M
06	MARIE/QUINQUENEAU	*MERE DE 02* (800)	r: FRANCE REGION INDETERMINEE		M	D	F
07	MARIE ANNE/FAYE	*SOEUR DE 02*					F
08	LOUIS/CHAMBALON	p:04					M

Figure 4-13

The date of the contract of marriage is shown in bold on the top line at the right. 1694-01-10.

There were eight (8) people mentioned in this marriage contract. This is indicated by the number 01 to 08 down the left side of the document.

01. Charles Branchereau, is the Groom. He is 28 years old (28 ans). He came from a rural area of western France, origin code 872. (o:FRANCE, OUEST, RURAL, (872)). He is single (C). He is male (M).

02. Anne Faye is the Bride. She resides in Québec (r: QUEBEC), origin code 451. She is single (C). She is female (F).

03. Jacques Bronchereau is the father of the groom (*PERE DE* 01). He is a carpenter (p: 51). He is male (M). He resides in rural, western France, origin code 872 (r: FRANCE, OUEST, RURAL, (872)).

04. Antoinette Vincent is the mother of the groom (*MERE DE* 01). She resided in rural, western France, origin code 872 (r: FRANCE, OUEST, RURAL, (872)). She is married (M). She is deceased (D). She is female (F).

05. Pierre Fay is the father of the bride (*PERE DE* 02). He resided in Québec, origin code 451 (r: QUEBEC, (451)). He is married (M). He is deceased (D). He is male (M).

06. Marie Quinqueneau is the mother of the bride (*MERE DE* 02). She resides somewhere in France, origin code 800 (r:FRANCE, REGION INDETERMINEE (800)). She is female (F).

07. Marie Anne Fay is the sister of the bride (*SOEUR DE* 02). She is female (F).

08. Louis Chambalon is the Notary (p:04). He is male (m).

Document - Hospital Sick List

		1699-07-19				
01	**MARIE FRANÇOISE/LEFÈBVRE**	28 ANS	r. QUÉBEC (451)	h: 1 JOUR		F
02	**MARIE/VALLE**	55 ANS	r. QUÉBEC (451)	h: 13 JOURS	M	F
03	/JOLICOEUR	*EPOUX DE* 02			M	M
04	**FRANÇOISE/LEFE**	50 ANS	r. CHARLESBOURG (465)	h: 13 JOURS	M	F
05	/PORTUGAIS	*EPOUX DE* 04				M
06	**ANDRE/CORBIN**	17 ANS	r. BEAUPORT	h: 13 JOURS		M
07	**JEAN/BOUDO**	50 ANS	r. CHARLESBOURG (465)	h: 13 JOURS		M
08	**JOSEPH/ANGLOIS**	12 ANS		h: 13 JOURS	C	M

Figure 4-14

The hospital sick list differs somewhat from the other documents in that it indicates the length of stay in the hospital as well as the age of the individual. The date on the document is the date of admission to the hospital. The names in bold print are the individuals admitted. The other names are family members.

01. **Marie Françoise Lefevre.** Marie is 28 years old (28 ANS). She is from Québec, source code 451 (r:QUÉBEC (451)). She was in the hospital for 1 day (h: 1 JOUR). She is female (F).

02. **Marie Vallé** Marie is 55 years old (55 ANS). She is a resident of Quebec, source code 451 (r: QUÉBEC (451). She was in the hospital for 13 days (13 JOURS). She is married (M). She is female (F).

03. **/Jolicoeur.** Mr Jolicoeur is the husband of Marie Valle (*EPOUX DE* 02). He is married (M). He is male (m).

04. **Françoise Lefe.** Francoise is 50 years old (50 ANS). She is a resident of Charlesbourg , source code 465 (r: Charlesbourg (465). She stayed in the hospital for 13 days (h: 13 JOURS). She is married (M). She is female (F).

05. **/Portugais.** Mr. Portugais is the husband of Francoise Lefe (*EPOUX DE 04*). He is married (M). He is male (M).

06. **André Corbin.** André is 17 years old (17 ANS). He is a resident of Beauport, source code 462 (r: BEAUPORT (462)). He was hospitalized for 13 days (h: 13 JOURS). He is male (M).

07. **Jean Boudo.** Jean is 50 years old (50 ANS). He is from Charlesbourg, source code 465 (r: CHARLESBOURG (465)). He was also in the hospital for 13 days (h: 13 JOURS). He is male (M).

08. **Joseph Anglois.** Joseph is 12 years old (12 ANS). He was in the hospital for 13 days , and is single (C), and male (M).

Document - Census Record

	1760	Ménage 13
01 CHARLES/BRANCHAUD	**P**	**M**

01 CHARLES/BRANCHAUD
- FEMME(S): 1
- ENFANT(S) DE SEXE MASCULIN: 4
- ENFANT(S) DE SEXE FEMININ: 3

Figure 4-15

The first line shows the date of the census (1760), and the number of the household in order of enumeration (13).

01 CHARLES/BRANCHAUD is printed in bold, indicating that he is the head of the household. He was present when the census was taken (P). He is a male (M).

FEMME(S):1 indicates that there was 1 adult female in the household.

ENFANT(S) DE SEXE MASCULIN: 4 indicates that there were 4 male children in the household.

ENFANT(S) DE SEXE FEMININ: 3 indicates that there were 3 female children in the household.

Notes:

CONTENTS OF THE PRDH BY VOLUME

VOLUME	SOURCE	DATE	NUMBER
01	NOTRE DAME DE QUEBEC	to 1699	451
02	CHATEAU RICHER	to 1699	382
02	L'ANGE GARDIEN	to 1699	384
02	ST ANNE DE BEAUPRE	to 1699	381
02	ST FAMILLE, I.O.	to 1699	383
02	ST FRANCOIS, I.O.	to 1699	387
02	ST JEAN, I.O.	to 1699	388
02	ST JOACHIM	to 1699	389
02	ST LAURENT, I.O.	to 1699	385
02	ST PIERRE, I.O.	to 1699	386
03	BAIE ST PAUL	to 1699	121
03	BEAUMONT	to 1699	061
03	BEAUPORT	to 1699	462
03	CAP SANTE	to 1699	441
03	CAP ST IGNACE	to 1699	372
03	CHARLESBOURG	to 1699	465
03	GRONDINES	to 1699	443
03	HOTEL DIEU DE QUEBEC	to 1699	452
03	L'ANCIENNE LORETTE	to 1699	463
03	L'ISLET	to 1699	311
03	LOTBINIERE	to 1699	321
03	NEUVILLE	to 1699	442
03	POINTE DE LEVIS	to 1699	301
03	POSTES DU DOMAINE DU ROI	to 1699	501
03	RIVIERE OUELLE	to 1699	251
03	SILLERY	to 1699	461
03	ST AUGUSTIN	to 1699	444
03	ST FOY	to 1699	466
03	ST MICHEL	to 1699	062
03	ST NICOLAS	to 1699	302
03	ST THOMAS	to 1699	371
04	BATISCAN	to 1699	113
04	CAP DE LA MADELEINE	to 1699	111
04	CHAMPLAIN	to 1699	112
04	ST ANNE DE LA PERADE	to 1699	114
04	ST FRANCOIS DU LAC	to 1699	631
04	TROIS RIVIERES	to 1699	601
05	BOUCHERVILLE	to 1699	101
05	CONTRECOEUR	to 1699	621
05	LACHENAIE	to 1699	282
05	LACHINE	to 1699	231
05	LAPRAIRIE	to 1699	271
05	LONGUEUIL	to 1699	102
05	MISSION D'L'ILE TOURTES	to 1699	236
05	MISSION DE LA MONTAGNE DE MONTREAL	to 1699	394

05	NOTRE DAME DE MONTREAL	to 1699	391
05	POINTE AUX TREMBLES	to 1699	191
05	REPENTIGNY	to 1699	281
05	RIVIERE DES PRAIRIES	to 1699	192
05	SOREL	to 1699	471
05	ST ANNE DU BOUT DE L'ILE	to 1699	232
05	VARENNES	to 1699	622
06	ABJURATIONS	to 1699	
06	ACTES TIRES DU JOURNAL DES JESUITES	to 1699	JSJ
06	ANNULATIONS DE MARIAGE	to 1699	
06		to 1699	NOT
06	ENGAGES DE LA ROCHELLE DU ST ANDRE	to 1699	871
06	ENGAGES DE LA ROCHELLE DU TAUREAU	to 1699	871
06	ENGAGES DE ST NAZAIRE	to 1699	812
06	HOPITAL GENERAL DE MONTREAL	to 1699	392
06	HOTEL DIEU DE QUEBEC	to 1699	452
06	RECENSEMENT DE 1666	1666	
06	RECENSEMENT DE 1667	1667	
06	RECENSEMENT DE 1681	1681	
06	RECENSEMENT DE MONT LOUIS DE 1699	to 1699	185
06	SOLDATS DU REGIMENT DE CARIGNAN	to 1699	000
07	GENERAL INDEX	to 1699	
08	HOPITAL GENERAL DE QUEBEC	1700-1729	453
08	HOTEL DIEU DE QUEBEC	1700-1729	452
08	NOTRE DAME DE QUEBEC	1700-1729	451
08	RECENSEMENT DE QUEBEC DE 1716	1700-1729	451
09	BAIE ST PAUL	1700-1729	121
09	CHATEAU RICHER	1700-1729	382
09	L'ANGE GARDIEN	1700-1729	384
09	POSTES DU DOMAINE DU ROI	1700-1729	501
09	ST ANNE DE BEAUPRE	1700-1729	381
09	ST FAMILLE, I.O.	1700-1729	383
09	ST FRANCOIS, I.O.	1700-1729	387
09	ST JEAN	1700-1729	388
09	ST JOACHIM	1700-1729	389
09	ST LAURENT, I.O.	1700-1729	385
09	ST PIERRE, I.O.	1700-1729	386
10	BEAUPORT	1700-1729	462
10	CAP SANTE	1700-1729	441
10	CHARLESBOURG	1700-1729	465
10	DESCHAMBAULT	1700-1729	445
10	GRONDINES	1700-1729	443
10	L'ANCIENNE LORETTE	1700-1729	463
10	NEUVILLE	1700-1729	442
10	ST AUGUSTIN	1700-1729	444
10	ST FOY	1700-1729	466

11	BEAUMONT	1700-1729	061
11	BERTHIER	1700-1729	373
11	CAP ST IGNACE	1700-1729	372
11	KAMOURASKA	1700-1729	253
11	L'ISLET	1700-1729	311
11	LOTBINIERE	1700-1729	321
11	MONT LOUIS	1700-1729	185
11	POINTE DE LEVIS	1700-1729	301
11	RECENSEMENT DE MONT LOUIS DE 1700	1700-1729	185
11	RIMOUSKI	1700-1729	481
11	RIVIERE OUELLE	1700-1729	251
11	ST ANNE DE LA POCATIERE	1700-1729	252
11	ST ANTOINE DE TILLY	1700-1729	323
11	ST CROIX	1700-1729	322
11	ST MICHEL	1700-1729	062
11	ST NICOLAS	1700-1729	302
11	ST PIERRE	1700-1729	375
11	ST THOMAS	1700-1729	371
11	ST VALLIER	1700-1729	063
11	TROIS PISTOLES	1700-1729	581
12	BAIE DU FEBVRE	1700-1729	632
12	BATISCAN	1700-1729	113
12	BECANCOUR	1700-1729	411
12	CAP DE LA MADELEINE	1700-1729	111
12	CHAMPLAIN	1700-1729	112
12	MASKINONGE	1700-1729	332
12	NICOLET	1700-1729	412
12	RIVIERE DU LOUP	1700-1729	331
12	ST ANNE DE LA PERADE	1700-1729	114
12	ST FRANCOIS DU LAC	1700-1729	631
12	ST GENEVIEVE DE BATISCAN	1700-1729	115
12	TROIS RIVIERES	1700-1729	601
12	YAMACHICHE	1700-1729	532
12	YAMASKA	1700-1729	633
13	HOPITAL GENERAL DE MONTREAL	1700-1729	392
13	NOTRE DAME DE MONTREAL	1700-1729	391
14	BERTHIER	1700-1729	073
14	ILE DUPAS	1700-1729	071
14	L'ASSOMPTION	1700-1729	284
14	LAC DES DEUX MONTAGNES	1700-1729	151
14	LACHENAIE	1700-1729	282
14	LACHINE	1700-1729	231
14	LONGUE POINTE	1700-1729	193
14	POINTE AUX TREMBLES	1700-1729	191
14	POINTE CLAIRE	1700-1729	233
14	REPENTIGNY	1700-1729	281
14	RIVIERE DES PRAIRIES	1700-1729	192
14	ST ANNE DE BOUT DE L'ILE	1700-1729	232
14	ST FRANCOIS DE SALES	1700-1729	291
14	ST LAURENT	1700-1729	234
14	ST SULPICE	1700-1729	283
14	TERREBONNE	1700-1729	591

15	BOUCHERVILLE	1700-1729	101
15	CHAMBLY	1700-1729	103
15	CONTRECOEUR	1700-1729	621
15	LAPRAIRIE	1700-1729	271
15	LONGUEUIL	1700-1729	102
15	SAULT ST LOUIS	1700-1729	272
15	SOREL	1700-1729	471
15	ST OURS	1700-1729	472
15	VARENNES	1700-1729	622
15	VERCHERES	1700-1729	623
16	GENERAL INDEX, VOLUMES 08-15, A-G	1700-1729	
17	GENERAL INDEX, VOLUMES 08-15, H-Z	1700-1729	
18	HOPITAL GENERAL DE QUEBEC	1730-1749	453
18	HOTEL DIEU DE QUEBEC	1730-1749	452
18	NOTRE DAME DE QUEBEC	1730-1749	451
18	RECENSEMENT DE QUEBEC 1744	1730-1749	451
19	BAIE ST PAUL	1730-1749	121
19	CHATEAU RICHER	1730-1749	382
19	ISLE AUX COUDRES	1730-1749	124
19	L'ANGE GARDIEN	1730-1749	384
19	LES EBOULEMENTS	1730-1749	122
19	PETITE RIVIERE ST FRANCOIS	1730-1749	123
19	POSTES DU DOMAINE DU ROI	1730-1749	501
19	ST ANNE DE BEAUPRE	1730-1749	381
19	ST FAMILLE, I.O.	1730-1749	383
19	ST FRANCOIS, I.O.	1730-1749	387
19	ST JEAN, I.O.	1730-1749	388
19	ST JOACHIM	1730-1749	389
19	ST LAURENT, I.O.	1730-1749	385
19	ST PIERRE, I.O.	1730-1749	386
20	BEAUPORT	1730-1749	462
20	CAP SANTE	1730-1749	441
20	CHARLESBOURG	1730-1749	465
20	DESCHAMBAULT	1730-1749	445
20	GRONDINES	1730-1749	443
20	L'ANCIENNE LORETTE	1730-1749	463
20	LES ECUREUILS	1730-1749	446
20	NEUVILLE	1730-1749	442
20	ST AUGUSTIN	1730-1749	444
20	ST FOY	1730-1749	466
21	BERTHIER	1730-1749	373
21	CAP ST IGNACE	1730-1749	372
21	KAMOURASKA	1730-1749	253
21	L'ISLET	1730-1749	311
21	RIMOUSKI	1730-1749	481
21	RIVIERE OUELLE	1730-1749	251
21	ST ANNE DE LA POCATIERE	1730-1749	252
21	ST FRANCOIS	1730-1749	374
21	ST PIERRE	1730-1749	375
21	ST ROCH DES AULNAIES	1730-1749	312
21	ST THOMAS	1730-1749	371
21	TROIS PISTOLES	1730-1749	581

22	BEAUMONT	1730-1749	061
22	DESCHAILLONS	1730-1749	324
22	LOTBINIERE	1730-1749	321
22	POINTE DE LEVIS	1730-1749	301
22	ST ANTOINE DE TILLY	1730-1749	323
22	ST CHARLES	1730-1749	064
22	ST CROIX	1730-1749	322
22	ST JOSEPH	1730-1749	041
22	ST MARIE	1730-1749	042
22	ST MICHEL	1730-1749	062
22	ST NICOLAS	1730-1749	302
22	ST VALLIER	1730-1749	063
23	BAIE DU FEBVRE	1730-1749	632
23	BATISCAN	1730-1749	113
23	BECANCOUR	1730-1749	411
23	CAP DE LA MADELEINE	1730-1749	111
23	CHAMPLAIN	1730-1749	112
23	FORGES DE ST MAURICE	1730-1749	533
23	MASKINONGE	1730-1749	332
23	NICOLET	1730-1749	412
23	POINTE DU LAC	1730-1749	531
23	RIVIERE DU LOUP	1730-1749	331
23	ST ANNE DE LA PERADE	1730-1749	114
23	ST FRANCOIS DU LAC	1730-1749	631
23	ST GENEVIEVE DE BATISCAN	1730-1749	115
23	ST PIERRE LES BECQUETS	1730-1749	413
23	TROIS RIVIERES	1730-1749	601
23	YAMACHICHE	1730-1749	532
23	YAMASKA	1730-1749	633
24	HOPITAL GENERAL DE MONTREAL	1730-1749	392
24	NOTRE DAME DE MONTREAL	1730-1749	391
25	LACHINE	1730-1749	231
25	LONGUE POINTE	1730-1749	193
25	POINTE AUX TREMBLES	1730-1749	191
25	POINTE CLAIRE	1730-1749	233
25	RIVIERE DES PRAIRIES	1730-1749	192
25	SAULT AU RECOLLET	1730-1749	195
25	ST ANNE DU BOUT DE L'ILE	1730-1749	232
25	ST GENEVIEVE	1730-1749	235
25	ST LAURENT	1730-1749	234
26	BERTHIER	1730-1749	073
26	ILE DUPAS	1730-1749	071
26	L'ASSOMPTION	1730-1749	284
26	LAC DES DEUX MONTAGNES	1730-1749	151
26	LACHENAIE	1730-1749	282
26	LANORAIE	1730-1749	074
26	LAVALTRIE	1730-1749	072
26	REPENTIGNY	1730-1749	281
26	ST FRANCOIS DE SALES	1730-1749	291
26	ST ROSE	1730-1749	293
26	ST SULPICE	1730-1749	283
26	ST VINCENT DE PAUL	1730-1749	292
26	TERREBONNE	1730-1749	591

27	CONTRECOEUR	1730-1749	621
27	POINTE OLIVIER	1730-1749	491
27	SOREL	1730-1749	471
27	ST CHARLES	1730-1749	511
27	ST DENIS	1730-1749	512
27	ST OURS	1730-1749	472
27	VARENNES	1730-1749	622
27	VERCHERES	1730-1749	623
28	BOUCHERVILLE	1730-1749	101
28	CHAMBLY	1730-1749	103
28	CHATEAUGUAY	1730-1749	131
28	LAPRAIRIE	1730-1749	271
28	LONGUEUIL	1730-1749	102
28	SAULT ST LOUIS	1730-1749	272
29	GENERAL INDEX, VOLUMES 18-28, A-G	1730-1749	
30	GENERAL INDEX, VOLUMES 18-28, H-Z	1730-1749	
31	HOPITAL GENERAL DE QUEBEC	1750-1765	453
31	HOTEL DIEU DE QUEBEC	1750-1765	452
31	NOTRE DAME DE QUEBEC	1750-1765	451
32	BAIE ST PAUL	1750-1765	121
32	CHATEAU RICHER	1750-1765	382
32	ISLE AUX COUDRES	1750-1765	124
32	L'ANGE GARDIEN	1750-1765	384
32	LES EBOULEMENTS	1750-1765	122
32	POSTES DU DOMAINE DU ROI	1750-1765	501
32	ST ANNE DE BEAUPRE	1750-1765	381
32	ST FAMILLE, I.O.	1750-1765	383
32	ST FRANCOIS, I.O.	1750-1765	387
32	ST JEAN, I.O.	1750-1765	388
32	ST JOACHIM	1750-1765	389
32	ST LAURENT, I.O.	1750-1765	385
32	ST PIERRE, I.O.	1750-1765	386
33	BEAUPORT	1750-1765	462
33	CAP SAINTE	1750-1765	441
33	CHARLESBOURG	1750-1765	465
33	DESCHAMBAULT	1750-1765	445
33	GRONDINES	1750-1765	443
33	L'ANCIENNE LORETTE	1750-1765	463
33	LES ECUREUILS	1750-1765	446
33	MISSION DES HURONS DE LA JEUNE LORETTE	1750-1765	464
33	NEUVILLE	1750-1765	442
33	ST AUGUSTIN	1750-1765	444
33	ST FOY	1750-1765	466

34	BERTHIER	1750-1765	373
34	CAP ST IGNACE	1750-1765	372
34	KAMOURASKA	1750-1765	253
34	L'ISLET	1750-1765	311
34	PABOS	1750-1765	182
34	RIMOUSKI	1750-1765	481
34	RISTIGOUCHE	1750-1765	081
34	RIVIERE OUELLE	1750-1765	251
34	ST ANNE DE LA POCATERIE	1750-1765	252
34	ST FRANCOIS	1750-1765	374
34	ST PIERRE	1750-1765	375
34	ST ROCH DES AULNAIES	1750-1765	312
34	ST THOMAS	1750-1765	371
34	TROIS PISTOLES	1750-1765	581
35	BEAUMONT	1750-1765	061
35	DESCHAILLONS	1750-1765	324
35	LOTBINIERE	1750-1765	321
35	POINTE DE LEVIS	1750-1765	301
35	POINTE DE LEVIS	1750-1765	331
35	ST ANTOINE DE TILLY	1750-1765	323
35	ST CHARLES	1750-1765	064
35	ST CROIX	1750-1765	322
35	ST FRANCOIS D'ASSISE	1750-1765	043
35	ST JOSEPH	1750-1765	041
35	ST MARIE	1750-1765	042
35	ST MICHEL	1750-1765	062
35	ST VALLIER	1750-1765	063
36	BAIE DU FEBVRE	1750-1765	632
36	BATISCAN	1750-1765	113
36	BECANCOUR	1750-1765	441
36	CAP DE LA MADELEINE	1750-1765	111
36	CHAMPLAIN	1750-1765	112
36	FORGES DE ST MAURICE	1750-1765	533
36	MASKINONGE	1750-1765	332
36	NICOLET	1750-1765	412
36	POINTE DU LAC	1750-1765	531
36	RIVIERE DU LOUP	1750-1765	331
36	ST ANNE DE LA PERADE	1750-1765	114
36	ST FRANCOIS DU LAC	1750-1765	631
36	ST GENEVIEVE DE BATISCAN	1750-1765	115
36	ST PIERRE LES BECQUETS	1750-1765	413
36	TROIS RIVIERES	1750-1765	601
36	YAMACHICHE	1750-1765	532
36	YAMASKA	1750-1765	633
37	HOPITAL GENERAL DE MONTREAL	1750-1765	392
37	HOTEL DIEU DE MONTREAL	1750-1765	393
37	NOTRE DAME DE MONTREAL	1750-1765	391
38	LACHINE	1750-1765	231
38	LONGUE POINTE	1750-1765	193
38	POINTE AUX TREMBLES	1750-1765	191
38	POINTE CLAIRE	1750-1765	233
38	RIVIERE DES PRAIRIES	1750-1765	192
38	SAULT AU RECOLLET	1750-1765	195
38	ST ANNE DU BOUT DE L'ILE	1750-1765	232
38	ST GENEVIEVE	1750-1765	235
38	ST LAURENT	1750-1765	234

39	BERTHIER	1750-1765	073
39	ILE DUPAS	1750-1765	071
39	L'ASSOMPTION	1750-1765	284
39	LACHENAIE	1750-1765	282
39	LANORAIE	1750-1765	074
39	LAVALTRIE	1750-1765	072
39	MASCOUCHE	1750-1765	285
39	REPENTIGNY	1750-1765	281
39	ST SULPICE	1750-1765	283
40	LAC DES DEUX MONTAGNES	1750-1765	151
40	SOULANGES	1750-1765	561
40	ST FRANCOIS DE SALES	1750-1765	291
40	ST ROSE	1750-1765	293
40	ST VINCENT DE PAUL	1750-1765	292
40	TERREBONNE	1750-1765	591
41	CONTRECOEUR	1750-1765	621
41	FORT ST JEAN	1750-1765	521
41	POINTE OLIVIER	1750-1765	491
41	SOREL	1750-1765	471
41	ST ANTOINE	1750-1765	624
41	ST CHARLES	1750-1765	511
41	ST DENIS	1750-1765	512
41	ST OURS	1750-1765	472
41	VARENNES	1750-1765	622
41	VERCHERES	1750-1765	623
42	BOUCHERVILLE	1750-1765	101
42	CHAMBLY	1750-1765	103
42	CHATEAUGUAY	1750-1765	131
42	LAPRAIRIE	1750-1765	271
42	LONGUEUIL	1750-1765	102
42	SAULT ST LOUIS	1750-1765	272
42	ST CONSTANT	1750-1765	273
42	ST PHILIPPE	1750-1765	274
42	ST REGIS	1750-1765	201
43	GENERAL INDEX, VOLUMES 31-42, A-D	1750-1765	
44	GENERAL INDEX, VOLUMES 31-42, E-L	1750-1765	
45	GENERAL INDEX, VOLUMES 31-42, M-Z	1750-1765	
46	POINTE DE LEVIS	1700-1765	301
46	ABJURATIONS	1700-1765	
46	ANNULATIONS DE MARIAGE	1700-1765	
46	BAIE DU FEBVRE	1700-1765	632
46	BAIE ST PAUL	1700-1765	121
46	BEAUMONT	1700-1765	161
46	BOUCHERVILLE	1700-1765	171
46	CAP SANTE	1700-1765	441
46	CAP ST IGNACE	1700-1765	372
46	CHAMBLY	1700-1765	103
46	CHAMPLAIN	1700-1765	112
46	CHARLESBOURG	1700-1765	465
46	CHATEAU RICHER	1700-1765	382

46	CONFIRMATIONS	1700-1765	
46	CONTRECOEUR	1700-1765	621
46	ENGAGES DE BORDEAUX	1700-1765	891
46	ENGAGES DE NANTES	1700-1765	811
46	HOPITAL GENERAL DE MONTREAL	1700-1765	392
46	HOTEL DIEU DE QUEBEC	1700-1765	452
46	ILE DUPAS	1700-1765	071
46	IMMIGRANTS: ENGAGES DE LA ROCHELLE	1700-1765	871
46	KAMOURASKA	1700-1765	253
46	L'ANCIENNE LORETTE	1700-1765	463
46	L'ANGE GARDIEN	1700-1765	384
46	L'ISLET	1700-1765	311
46	LAC DES DEUX MONTAGNES	1700-1765	151
46	LACHENAIE	1700-1765	282
46	LACHINE	1700-1765	231
46	LANORAIE	1700-1765	074
46	LAPRAIRIE	1700-1765	271
46	LIST OF IMMIGRANTS: FAUX SAUNIERS	1700-1765	800
46	LOTBINIERE	1700-1765	321
46	MONTREAL	1700-1765	391
46	NATURALIZATIONS	1700-1765	
46	PETITE RIVIERE ST FRANCOIS	1700-1765	123
46	POINTE AUX TREMBLES	1700-1765	191
46	POSTES DU DOMAINE DU ROI	1700-1765	501
46	QUEBEC	1700-1765	451
46	REINSTATED MARRIAGES	1700-1765	
46	SOREL	1700-1765	471
46	ST ANNE DE LA PERADE	1700-1765	114
46	ST ANNE DE LA POCATIERE	1700-1765	252
46	ST ANTOINE DE TILLY	1700-1765	323
46	ST AUGUSTIN	1700-1765	444
46	ST CROIX	1700-1765	322
46	ST FOY	1700-1765	466
46	ST FRANCOIS DU LAC	1700-1765	631
46	ST FRANCOIS, I.O.	1700-1765	387
46	ST GENEVIEVE	1700-1765	235
46	ST GENEVIEVE DE BATISCAN	1700-1765	115
46	ST JEAN, I.O.	1700-1765	388
46	ST MARIE	1700-1765	042
46	ST NICOLAS	1700-1765	302
46	ST PIERRE, I.O.	1700-1765	386
46	ST ROCH DES AULNAIES	1700-1765	312
46	ST ROSE	1700-1765	293
46	ST SULPICE	1700-1765	283
46	ST THOMAS	1700-1765	371
46	ST VALLIER	1700-1765	063
46	TERREBONNE	1700-1765	591
46	TROIS RIVIERES	1700-1765	601
46	WITNESSES WHO TESTIFIED IN ANNULMENTS	1700-1765	
47	GENERAL INDEX	1700-1765	
47	RECENSEMENT DE 1765	1700-1765	
47	RECENSEMENT DE QUEBEC, 1762	1700-1765	
47	RECENSEMENT DE TROIS RIVIERES, 1760	1700-1765	

CONTENTS OF THE PRDH BY SOURCE NUMBER

NUMBER	SOURCE	DATE	VOLUME
	ABJURATIONS	to 1699	06
	ABJURATIONS	1700-1765	46
	ANNULATIONS DE MARIAGE	to 1699	06
	ANNULATIONS DE MARIAGE	1700-1765	46
	CONFIRMATIONS	1700-1765	46
	GENERAL INDEX	to 1699	07
	GENERAL INDEX	1700-1765	47
	GENERAL INDEX, VOLUMES 08-15, A-G	1700-1729	16
	GENERAL INDEX, VOLUMES 08-15, H-Z	1700-1729	17
	GENERAL INDEX, VOLUMES 18-28, A-G	1730-1749	29
	GENERAL INDEX, VOLUMES 18-28, H-Z	1730-1749	30
	GENERAL INDEX, VOLUMES 31-42, A-D	1750-1765	43
	GENERAL INDEX, VOLUMES 31-42, E-L	1750-1765	44
	GENERAL INDEX, VOLUMES 31-42, M-Z	1750-1765	45
	NATURALIZATIONS	1700-1765	46
	RECENSEMENT DE 1666	1666	06
	RECENSEMENT DE 1667	1667	06
	RECENSEMENT DE 1681	1681	06
	RECENSEMENT DE 1765	1700-1765	47
	RECENSEMENT DE QUEBEC, 1762	1700-1765	47
	RECENSEMENT DE TROIS RIVIERES, 1760	1700-1765	47
	REINSTATED MARRIAGES	1700-1765	46
	WITNESSES WHO TESTIFIED IN ANNULMENTS	1700-1765	46
000	SOLDATS DU REGIMENT DE CARIGNAN	to 1699	06
041	ST JOSEPH	1730-1749	22
041	ST JOSEPH	1750-1765	35
042	ST MARIE	1730-1749	22
042	ST MARIE	1750-1765	35
042	ST MARIE	1700-1765	46

043	ST FRANCOIS D'ASSISE	1750-1765	35
061	BEAUMONT	to 1699	03
061	BEAUMONT	1700-1729	11
061	BEAUMONT	1730-1749	22
061	BEAUMONT	1750-1765	35
062	ST MICHEL	to 1699	03
062	ST MICHEL	1700-1729	11
062	ST MICHEL	1730-1749	22
062	ST MICHEL	1750-1765	35
063	ST VALLIER	1700-1729	11
063	ST VALLIER	1730-1749	22
063	ST VALLIER	1750-1765	35
063	ST VALLIER	1700-1765	46
064	ST CHARLES	1730-1749	22
064	ST CHARLES	1750-1765	35
071	ILE DUPAS	1700-1729	14
071	ILE DUPAS	1730-1749	26
071	ILE DUPAS	1750-1765	39
071	ILE DUPAS	1700-1765	46
072	LAVALTRIE	1730-1749	26
072	LAVALTRIE	1750-1765	39
073	BERTHIER	1700-1729	14
073	BERTHIER	1730-1749	26
073	BERTHIER	1750-1765	39
074	LANORAIE	1730-1749	26
074	LANORAIE	1750-1765	39
074	LANORAIE	1700-1765	46
081	RISTIGOUCHE	1750-1765	34
101	BOUCHERVILLE	to 1699	05
101	BOUCHERVILLE	1700-1729	15
101	BOUCHERVILLE	1730-1749	28
101	BOUCHERVILLE	1750-1765	42
102	LONGUEUIL	to 1699	05
102	LONGUEUIL	1700-1729	15
102	LONGUEUIL	1730-1749	28
102	LONGUEUIL	1750-1765	42
103	CHAMBLY	1700-1729	15
103	CHAMBLY	1730-1749	28
103	CHAMBLY	1750-1765	42
103	CHAMBLY	1700-1765	46

111	CAP DE LA MADELEINE	to 1699	04
111	CAP DE LA MADELEINE	1700-1729	12
111	CAP DE LA MADELEINE	1730-1749	23
111	CAP DE LA MADELEINE	1750-1765	36
112	CHAMPLAIN	to 1699	04
112	CHAMPLAIN	1700-1729	12
112	CHAMPLAIN	1730-1749	23
112	CHAMPLAIN	1750-1765	36
112	CHAMPLAIN	1700-1765	46
113	BATISCAN	to 1699	04
113	BATISCAN	1700-1729	12
113	BATISCAN	1730-1749	23
113	BATISCAN	1750-1765	36
114	ST ANNE DE LA PERADE	to 1699	04
114	ST ANNE DE LA PERADE	1700-1729	12
114	ST ANNE DE LA PERADE	1730-1749	23
114	ST ANNE DE LA PERADE	1750-1765	36
114	ST ANNE DE LA PERADE	1700-1765	46
115	ST GENEVIEVE DE BATISCAN	1700-1729	12
115	ST GENEVIEVE DE BATISCAN	1730-1749	23
115	ST GENEVIEVE DE BATISCAN	1750-1765	36
115	ST GENEVIEVE DE BATISCAN	1700-1765	46
121	BAIE ST PAUL	to 1699	03
121	BAIE ST PAUL	1700-1729	09
121	BAIE ST PAUL	1730-1749	19
121	BAIE ST PAUL	1750-1765	31
121	BAIE ST PAUL	1700-1765	46
122	LES EBOULEMENTS	1730-1749	19
122	LES EBOULEMENTS	1750-1765	32
123	PETITE RIVIERE ST FRANCOIS	1730-1749	19
123	PETITE RIVIERE ST FRANCOIS	1700-1765	46
124	ISLE AUX COUDRES	1730-1749	19
124	ISLE AUX COUDRES	1750-1765	32
131	CHATEAUGUAY	1730-1749	28
131	CHATEAUGUAY	1750-1765	42
151	LAC DES DEUX MONTAGNES	1700-1729	14
151	LAC DES DEUX MONTAGNES	1730-1749	26
151	LAC DES DEUX MONTAGNES	1750-1765	40
151	LAC DES DEUX MONTAGNES	1700-1765	46
161	BEAUMONT	1700-1765	46
171	BOUCHERVILLE	1700-1765	46

182	PABOS	1750-1765	34
185	RECENSEMENT DE MONT LOUIS DE 1699	to 1699	06
185	MONT LOUIS	1700-1729	11
185	RECENSEMENT DE MONT LOUIS DE 1700	1700-1729	11
191	POINTE AUX TREMBLES	to 1699	05
191	POINTE AUX TREMBLES	1700-1729	14
191	POINTE AUX TREMBLES	1730-1749	25
191	POINTE AUX TREMBLES	1750-1765	38
191	POINTE AUX TREMBLES	1700-1765	46
192	RIVIERE DES PRAIRIES	to 1699	05
192	RIVIERE DES PRAIRIES	1700-1729	14
192	RIVIERE DES PRAIRIES	1730-1749	25
192	RIVIERE DES PRAIRIES	1750-1765	38
193	LONGUE POINTE	1700-1729	14
193	LONGUE POINTE	1730-1749	25
193	LONGUE POINTE	1750-1765	38
195	SAULT AU RECOLLET	1730-1749	25
195	SAULT AU RECOLLET	1750-1765	38
201	ST REGIS	1750-1765	42
231	LACHINE	to 1699	05
231	LACHINE	1700-1729	14
231	LACHINE	1730-1749	25
231	LACHINE	1750-1765	38
231	LACHINE	1700-1765	46
232	ST ANNE DE BOUT DE L'ILE	1700-1729	14
232	ST ANNE DU BOUT DE L'ILE	to 1699	05
232	ST ANNE DU BOUT DE L'ILE	1730-1749	25
232	ST ANNE DU BOUT DE L'ILE	1750-1765	38
233	POINTE CLAIRE	1700-1729	14
233	POINTE CLAIRE	1730-1749	25
233	POINTE CLAIRE	1750-1765	38
234	ST LAURENT	1700-1729	14
234	ST LAURENT	1730-1749	25
234	ST LAURENT	1750-1765	38
235	ST GENEVIEVE	1730-1749	25
235	ST GENEVIEVE	1750-1765	38
235	ST GENEVIEVE	1700-1765	46
236	MISSION D'L'ILE TOURTES	to 1699	05
251	RIVIERE OUELLE	to 1699	03
251	RIVIERE OUELLE	1700-1729	11
251	RIVIERE OUELLE	1730-1749	21
251	RIVIERE OUELLE	1750-1765	34

252	ST ANNE DE LA POCATIERE	1700-1729	11
252	ST ANNE DE LA POCATIERE	1730-1749	21
252	ST ANNE DE LA POCATERIE	1750-1765	34
252	ST ANNE DE LA POCATIERE	1700-1765	46
253	KAMOURASKA	1700-1729	11
253	KAMOURASKA	1730-1749	21
253	KAMOURASKA	1750-1765	34
253	KAMOURASKA	1700-1765	46
271	LAPRAIRIE	to 1699	05
271	LAPRAIRIE	1700-1729	15
271	LAPRAIRIE	1730-1749	28
271	LAPRAIRIE	1750-1765	42
271	LAPRAIRIE	1700-1765	46
272	SAULT ST LOUIS	1700-1729	15
272	SAULT ST LOUIS	1730-1749	28
272	SAULT ST LOUIS	1750-1765	42
273	ST CONSTANT	1750-1765	42
274	ST PHILIPPE	1750-1765	42
281	REPENTIGNY	to 1699	05
281	REPENTIGNY	1700-1729	14
281	REPENTIGNY	1730-1749	26
281	REPENTIGNY	1750-1765	39
282	LACHENAIE	to 1699	05
282	LACHENAIE	1700-1729	14
282	LACHENAIE	1730-1749	26
282	LACHENAIE	1750-1765	39
282	LACHENAIE	1700-1765	46
283	ST SULPICE	1700-1729	14
283	ST SULPICE	1730-1749	26
283	ST SULPICE	1750-1765	39
283	ST SULPICE	1700-1765	46
284	L'ASSOMPTION	1700-1729	14
284	L'ASSOMPTION	1730-1749	26
284	L'ASSOMPTION	1750-1765	39
285	MASCOUCHE	1750-1765	39
291	ST FRANCOIS DE SALES	1700-1729	14
291	ST FRANCOIS DE SALES	1730-1749	26
291	ST FRANCOIS DE SALES	1750-1765	40
292	ST VINCENT DE PAUL	1730-1749	26
292	ST VINCENT DE PAUL	1750-1765	40

293	ST ROSE	1730-1749	26
293	ST ROSE	1750-1765	40
293	ST ROSE	1700-1765	46
301	POINTE DE LEVIS	to 1699	03
301	POINTE DE LEVIS	1700-1729	11
301	POINTE DE LEVIS	1730-1749	22
301	POINTE DE LEVIS	1750-1765	35
301	POINTE DE LEVIS	1700-1765	46
302	ST NICOLAS	to 1699	03
302	ST NICOLAS	1700-1729	11
302	ST NICOLAS	1730-1749	22
302	ST NICOLAS	1700-1765	46
311	L'ISLET	to 1699	03
311	L'ISLET	1700-1729	11
311	L'ISLET	1730-1749	21
311	L'ISLET	1750-1765	34
311	L'ISLET	1700-1765	46
312	ST ROCH DES AULNAIES	1730-1749	21
312	ST ROCH DES AULNAIES	1750-1765	34
312	ST ROCH DES AULNAIES	1700-1765	46
321	LOTBINIERE	to 1699	03
321	LOTBINIERE	1700-1729	11
321	LOTBINIERE	1730-1749	22
321	LOTBINIERE	1750-1765	35
321	LOTBINIERE	1700-1765	46
322	ST CROIX	1700-1729	11
322	ST CROIX	1730-1749	22
322	ST CROIX	1750-1765	35
322	ST CROIX	1700-1765	46
323	ST ANTOINE DE TILLY	1700-1729	11
323	ST ANTOINE DE TILLY	1730-1749	22
323	ST ANTOINE DE TILLY	1750-1765	35
323	ST ANTOINE DE TILLY	1700-1765	46
324	DESCHAILLONS	1730-1749	22
324	DESCHAILLONS	1750-1765	35
331	POINTE DE LEVIS	1750-1765	35
331	RIVIERE DU LOUP	1700-1729	12
331	RIVIERE DU LOUP	1730-1749	23
331	RIVIERE DU LOUP	1750-1765	36
332	MASKINONGE	1700-1729	12
332	MASKINONGE	1730-1749	23
332	MASKINONGE	1750-1765	36

371	ST THOMAS	to 1699	03
371	ST THOMAS	1700-1729	11
371	ST THOMAS	1730-1749	21
371	ST THOMAS	1750-1765	34
371	ST THOMAS	1700-1765	46
372	CAP ST IGNACE	to 1699	03
372	CAP ST IGNACE	1700-1729	11
372	CAP ST IGNACE	1730-1749	21
372	CAP ST IGNACE	1750-1765	34
372	CAP ST IGNACE	1700-1765	46
373	BERTHIER	1700-1729	11
373	BERTHIER	1730-1749	21
373	BERTHIER	1750-1765	34
374	ST FRANCOIS	1730-1749	21
374	ST FRANCOIS	1750-1765	34
375	ST PIERRE	1700-1729	11
375	ST PIERRE	1730-1749	21
375	ST PIERRE	1750-1765	34
381	ST ANNE DE BEAUPRE	to 1699	02
381	ST ANNE DE BEAUPRE	1700-1729	09
381	ST ANNE DE BEAUPRE	1730-1749	19
381	ST ANNE DE BEAUPRE	1750-1765	32
382	CHATEAU RICHER	to 1699	02
382	CHATEAU RICHER	1700-1729	09
382	CHATEAU RICHER	1730-1749	19
382	CHATEAU RICHER	1750-1765	32
382	CHATEAU RICHER	1700-1765	46
383	ST FAMILLE, I.O.	to 1699	02
383	ST FAMILLE, I.O.	1700-1729	09
383	ST FAMILLE, I.O.	1730-1749	19
383	ST FAMILLE, I.O.	1750-1765	32
384	L'ANGE GARDIEN	to 1699	02
384	L'ANGE GARDIEN	1700-1729	09
384	L'ANGE GARDIEN	1730-1749	19
384	L'ANGE GARDIEN	1750-1765	32
384	L'ANGE GARDIEN	1700-1765	46
385	ST LAURENT, I.O.	to 1699	02
385	ST LAURENT, I.O.	1700-1729	09
385	ST LAURENT, I.O.	1730-1749	19
385	ST LAURENT, I.O.	1750-1765	32
386	ST PIERRE, I.O.	to 1699	02
386	ST PIERRE, I.O.	1700-1729	09
386	ST PIERRE, I.O.	1730-1749	19
386	ST PIERRE, I.O.	1750-1765	32
386	ST PIERRE, I.O.	1700-1765	46

387	ST FRANCOIS, I.O.	to 1699	02
387	ST FRANCOIS, I.O.	1700-1729	09
387	ST FRANCOIS, I.O.	1730-1749	19
387	ST FRANCOIS, I.O.	1750-1765	32
387	ST FRANCOIS, I.O.	1700-1765	46
388	ST JEAN, I.O.	to 1699	02
388	ST JEAN, I.O.	1700-1729	09
388	ST JEAN, I.O.	1730-1749	19
388	ST JEAN, I.O.	1750-1765	32
388	ST JEAN, I.O.	1700-1765	46
389	ST JOACHIM	to 1699	02
389	ST JOACHIM	1700-1729	09
389	ST JOACHIM	1730-1749	19
389	ST JOACHIM	1750-1765	32
391	MONTREAL	1700-1765	46
391	NOTRE DAME DE MONTREAL	to 1699	05
391	NOTRE DAME DE MONTREAL	1700-1729	13
391	NOTRE DAME DE MONTREAL	1730-1749	24
391	NOTRE DAME DE MONTREAL	1750-1765	37
392	HOPITAL GENERAL DE MONTREAL	to 1699	06
392	HOPITAL GENERAL DE MONTREAL	1700-1729	13
392	HOPITAL GENERAL DE MONTREAL	1730-1749	24
392	HOPITAL GENERAL DE MONTREAL	1750-1765	37
392	HOPITAL GENERAL DE MONTREAL	1700-1765	46
393	HOTEL DIEU DE MONTREAL	1750-1765	37
394	MISSION DE LA MONTAGNE DE MONTREAL	to 1699	05
411	BECANCOUR	1700-1729	12
411	BECANCOUR	1730-1749	23
411	BECANCOUR	1750-1765	36
412	NICOLET	1700-1729	12
412	NICOLET	1730-1749	23
412	NICOLET	1750-1765	36
413	ST PIERRE LES BECQUETS	1730-1749	23
413	ST PIERRE LES BECQUETS	1750-1765	36
441	CAP SANTE	to 1699	03
441	CAP SANTE	1700-1729	10
441	CAP SANTE	1730-1749	20
441	CAP SAINTE	1750-1765	33
441	CAP SANTE	1700-1765	46
442	NEUVILLE	to 1699	03
442	NEUVILLE	1700-1729	10
442	NEUVILLE	1730-1749	20
442	NEUVILLE	1750-1765	33

443	GRONDINES	to 1699	03
443	GRONDINES	1700-1729	10
443	GRONDINES	1730-1749	20
443	GRONDINES	1750-1765	33
444	ST AUGUSTIN	to 1699	03
444	ST AUGUSTIN	1700-1729	10
444	ST AUGUSTIN	1730-1749	20
444	ST AUGUSTIN	1750-1765	33
444	ST AUGUSTIN	1700-1765	46
445	DESCHAMBAULT	1700-1729	10
445	DESCHAMBAULT	1730-1749	20
445	DESCHAMBAULT	1750-1765	33
446	LES ECUREUILS	1730-1749	20
446	LES ECUREUILS	1750-1765	33
451	NOTRE DAME DE QUEBEC	to 1699	01
451	NOTRE DAME DE QUEBEC	1700-1729	08
451	NOTRE DAME DE QUEBEC	1730-1749	18
451	NOTRE DAME DE QUEBEC	1750-1765	31
451	QUEBEC	1700-1765	46
451	RECENSEMENT DE QUEBEC DE 1716	1700-1729	08
451	RECENSEMENT DE QUEBEC 1744	1730-1749	18
452	HOTEL DIEU DE QUEBEC	to 1699	03
452	HOTEL DIEU DE QUEBEC, LISTE DE MALADE	to 1699	06
452	HOTEL DIEU DE QUEBEC	1700-1729	08
452	HOTEL DIEU DE QUEBEC	1730-1749	18
452	HOTEL DIEU DE QUEBEC	1750-1765	31
452	HOTEL DIEU DE QUEBEC	1700-1765	46
453	HOPITAL GENERAL DE QUEBEC	1700-1729	08
453	HOPITAL GENERAL DE QUEBEC	1730-1749	18
453	HOPITAL GENERAL DE QUEBEC	1750-1765	31
461	SILLERY	to 1699	03
462	BEAUPORT	to 1699	03
462	BEAUPORT	1700-1729	10
462	BEAUPORT	1730-1749	20
462	BEAUPORT	1750-1765	33
463	L'ANCIENNE LORETTE	to 1699	03
463	L'ANCIENNE LORETTE	1700-1729	10
463	L'ANCIENNE LORETTE	1730-1749	20
463	L'ANCIENNE LORETTE	1750-1765	33
463	L'ANCIENNE LORETTE	1700-1765	46
464	MISSION DES HURONS DE LA JEUNE LORETTE	1750-1765	33

465	CHARLESBOURG	to 1699	03
465	CHARLESBOURG	1700-1729	10
465	CHARLESBOURG	1730-1749	20
465	CHARLESBOURG	1750-1765	33
465	CHARLESBOURG	1700-1765	46
466	ST FOY	to 1699	03
466	ST FOY	1700-1729	10
466	ST FOY	1730-1749	20
466	ST FOY	1750-1765	33
466	ST FOY	1700-1765	46
471	SOREL	to 1699	05
471	SOREL	1700-1729	15
471	SOREL	1730-1749	27
471	SOREL	1750-1765	41
471	SOREL	1700-1765	46
472	ST OURS	1700-1729	15
472	ST OURS	1730-1749	27
472	ST OURS	1750-1765	41
481	RIMOUSKI	1700-1729	11
481	RIMOUSKI	1730-1749	21
481	RIMOUSKI	1750-1765	34
491	POINTE OLIVIER	1730-1749	27
491	POINTE OLIVIER	1750-1765	41
501	POSTES DU DOMAINE DU ROI	to 1699	03
501	POSTES DU DOMAINE DU ROI	1700-1729	09
501	POSTES DU DOMAINE DU ROI	1730-1749	19
501	POSTES DU DOMAINE DU ROI	1750-1765	32
501	POSTES DU DOMAINE DU ROI	1700-1765	46
511	ST CHARLES	1730-1749	27
511	ST CHARLES	1750-1765	41
512	ST DENIS	1730-1749	27
512	ST DENIS	1750-1765	41
521	FORT ST JEAN	1750-1765	41
531	POINTE DU LAC	1730-1749	23
531	POINTE DU LAC	1750-1765	36
532	YAMACHICHE	1700-1729	12
532	YAMACHICHE	1730-1749	23
532	YAMACHICHE	1750-1765	36
533	FORGES DE ST MAURICE	1730-1749	23
533	FORGES DE ST MAURICE	1750-1765	36

561	SOULANGES	1750-1765	40
581	TROIS PISTOLES	1700-1729	11
581	TROIS PISTOLES	1730-1749	21
581	TROIS PISTOLES	1750-1765	34
591	TERREBONNE	1700-1729	14
591	TERREBONNE	1730-1749	26
591	TERREBONNE	1750-1765	40
591	TERREBONNE	1700-1765	46
601	TROIS RIVIERES	to 1699	04
601	TROIS RIVIERES	1700-1729	12
601	TROIS RIVIERES	1730-1749	23
601	TROIS RIVIERES	1750-1765	36
601	TROIS RIVIERES	1700-1765	46
621	CONTRECOEUR	to 1699	05
621	CONTRECOEUR	1700-1729	15
621	CONTRECOEUR	1730-1749	27
621	CONTRECOEUR	1750-1765	41
621	CONTRECOEUR	1700-1765	46
622	VARENNES	to 1699	05
622	VARENNES	1700-1729	15
622	VARENNES	1730-1749	27
622	VARENNES	1750-1765	41
623	VERCHERES	1700-1729	15
623	VERCHERES	1730-1749	27
623	VERCHERES	1750-1765	41
624	ST ANTOINE	1750-1765	41
631	ST FRANCOIS DU LAC	to 1699	04
631	ST FRANCOIS DU LAC	1700-1729	12
631	ST FRANCOIS DU LAC	1730-1749	23
631	ST FRANCOIS DU LAC	1750-1765	36
631	ST FRANCOIS DU LAC	1700-1765	46
632	BAIE DU FEBVRE	1700-1729	12
632	BAIE DU FEBVRE	1730-1749	23
632	BAIE DU FEBVRE	1750-1765	36
632	BAIE DU FEBVRE	1700-1765	46
633	YAMASKA	1700-1729	12
633	YAMASKA	1730-1749	23
633	YAMASKA	1750-1765	36

CONTENTS OF THE PRDH BY SOURCE

SOURCE	DATE	NUMBER	VOLUME
ABJURATIONS	to 1699		06
ABJURATIONS	1700-1765		46
ACTES TIRES DU JOURNAL DES JESUITES	to 1699	JSJ	06
ANNULATIONS DE MARIAGE	to 1699		06
ANNULATIONS DE MARIAGE	1700-1765		46
BAIE DU FEBVRE	1700-1729	632	12
BAIE DU FEBVRE	1700-1765	632	46
BAIE DU FEBVRE	1730-1749	632	23
BAIE DU FEBVRE	1750-1765	632	36
BAIE ST PAUL	to 1699	121	03
BAIE ST PAUL	1700-1729	121	09
BAIE ST PAUL	1730-1749	121	19
BAIE ST PAUL	1750-1765	121	31
BAIE ST PAUL	1700-1765	121	46
BATISCAN	to 1699	113	04
BATISCAN	1700-1729	113	12
BATISCAN	1730-1749	113	23
BATISCAN	1750-1765	113	36
BEAUMONT	to 1699	061	03
BEAUMONT	1700-1729	061	11
BEAUMONT	1730-1749	061	22
BEAUMONT	1750-1765	061	35
BEAUMONT	1700-1765	161	46
BEAUPORT	to 1699	462	03
BEAUPORT	1700-1729	462	10
BEAUPORT	1730-1749	462	20
BEAUPORT	1750-1765	462	33
BECANCOUR	1700-1729	411	12
BECANCOUR	1730-1749	411	23
BECANCOUR	1750-1765	441	36
BERTHIER	1700-1729	373	11
BERTHIER	1700-1729	073	14
BERTHIER	1730-1749	373	21
BERTHIER	1730-1749	073	26
BERTHIER	1750-1765	373	34
BERTHIER	1750-1765	073	39

BOUCHERVILLE	to 1699	101	05
BOUCHERVILLE	1700-1729	101	15
BOUCHERVILLE	1730-1749	101	28
BOUCHERVILLE	1750-1765	101	42
BOUCHERVILLE	1700-1765	171	46
CAP DE LA MADELEINE	to 1699	111	04
CAP DE LA MADELEINE	1700-1729	111	12
CAP DE LA MADELEINE	1730-1749	111	23
CAP DE LA MADELEINE	1750-1765	111	36
CAP SAINTE	1750-1765	441	33
CAP SANTE	to 1699	441	03
CAP SANTE	1700-1729	441	10
CAP SANTE	1730-1749	441	20
CAP SANTE	1700-1765	441	46
CAP ST IGNACE	to 1699	372	03
CAP ST IGNACE	1700-1729	372	11
CAP ST IGNACE	1730-1749	372	21
CAP ST IGNACE	1750-1765	372	34
CAP ST IGNACE	1700-1765	372	46
CHAMBLY	1700-1729	103	15
CHAMBLY	1730-1749	103	28
CHAMBLY	1750-1765	103	42
CHAMBLY	1700-1765	103	46
CHAMPLAIN	to 1699	112	04
CHAMPLAIN	1700-1729	112	12
CHAMPLAIN	1730-1749	112	23
CHAMPLAIN	1750-1765	112	36
CHAMPLAIN	1700-1765	112	46
CHARLESBOURG	to 1699	465	03
CHARLESBOURG	1700-1729	465	10
CHARLESBOURG	1730-1749	465	20
CHARLESBOURG	1750-1765	465	33
CHARLESBOURG	1700-1765	465	46
CHATEAU RICHER	to 1699	382	02
CHATEAU RICHER	1700-1729	382	09
CHATEAU RICHER	1730-1749	382	19
CHATEAU RICHER	1750-1765	382	32
CHATEAU RICHER	1700-1765	382	46
CHATEAUGUAY	1730-1749	131	28
CHATEAUGUAY	1750-1765	131	42
CONFIRMATIONS	1700-1765		46
CONTRATS DE MARIAGE	to 1699	NOT	06

CONTRECOEUR	to 1699	621	05
CONTRECOEUR	1700-1729	621	15
CONTRECOEUR	1730-1749	621	27
CONTRECOEUR	1750-1765	621	41
CONTRECOEUR	1700-1765	621	46
DESCHAILLONS	1730-1749	324	22
DESCHAILLONS	1750-1765	324	35
DESCHAMBAULT	1700-1729	445	10
DESCHAMBAULT	1730-1749	445	20
DESCHAMBAULT	1750-1765	445	33
ENGAGES DE BORDEAUX	1700-1765	891	46
ENGAGES DE LA ROCHELLE DU ST ANDRE	to 1699	871	06
ENGAGES DE LA ROCHELLE DU TAUREAU	to 1699	871	06
ENGAGES DE NANTES	1700-1765	811	46
ENGAGES DE ST NAZAIRE	to 1699	812	06
FORGES DE ST MAURICE	1730-1749	533	23
FORGES DE ST MAURICE	1750-1765	533	36
FORT ST JEAN	1750-1765	521	41
GENERAL INDEX	to 1699		07
GENERAL INDEX	1700-1765		47
GENERAL INDEX, VOLUMES 08-15, A-G	1700-1729		16
GENERAL INDEX, VOLUMES 08-15, H-Z	1700-1729		17
GENERAL INDEX, VOLUMES 18-28, A-G	1730-1749		29
GENERAL INDEX, VOLUMES 18-28, H-Z	1730-1749		30
GENERAL INDEX, VOLUMES 31-42, A-D	1750-1765		43
GENERAL INDEX, VOLUMES 31-42, E-L	1750-1765		44
GENERAL INDEX, VOLUMES 31-42, M-Z	1750-1765		45
GRONDINES	to 1699	443	03
GRONDINES	1700-1729	443	10
GRONDINES	1730-1749	443	20
GRONDINES	1750-1765	443	33

HOPITAL GENERAL DE MONTREAL	to 1699	392	06
HOPITAL GENERAL DE MONTREAL	1700-1729	392	13
HOPITAL GENERAL DE MONTREAL	1730-1749	392	24
HOPITAL GENERAL DE MONTREAL	1750-1765	392	37
HOPITAL GENERAL DE MONTREAL	1700-1765	392	46
HOPITAL GENERAL DE QUEBEC	1700-1729	453	08
HOPITAL GENERAL DE QUEBEC	1730-1749	453	18
HOPITAL GENERAL DE QUEBEC	1750-1765	453	31
HOTEL DIEU DE MONTREAL	1750-1765	393	37
HOTEL DIEU DE QUEBEC	to 1699	452	03
HOTEL DIEU DE QUEBEC, LISTE DE MALADE	to 1699	452	06
HOTEL DIEU DE QUEBEC	1700-1729	452	08
HOTEL DIEU DE QUEBEC	1730-1749	452	18
HOTEL DIEU DE QUEBEC	1750-1765	452	31
HOTEL DIEU DE QUEBEC	1700-1765	452	46
ILE DUPAS	1700-1729	071	14
ILE DUPAS	1730-1749	071	26
ILE DUPAS	1750-1765	071	39
ILE DUPAS	1700-1765	071	46
IMMIGRANTS: ENGAGES DE LA ROCHELLE	1700-1765	871	46
ISLE AUX COUDRES	1730-1749	124	19
ISLE AUX COUDRES	1750-1765	124	32
KAMOURASKA	1700-1729	253	11
KAMOURASKA	1730-1749	253	21
KAMOURASKA	1750-1765	253	34
KAMOURASKA	1700-1765	253	46
LAC DES DEUX MONTAGNES	1700-1729	151	14
LAC DES DEUX MONTAGNES	1730-1749	151	26
LAC DES DEUX MONTAGNES	1750-1765	151	40
LAC DES DEUX MONTAGNES	1700-1765	151	46
LACHENAIE	to 1699	282	05
LACHENAIE	1700-1729	282	14
LACHENAIE	1730-1749	282	26
LACHENAIE	1750-1765	282	39
LACHENAIE	1700-1765	282	46
LACHINE	to 1699	231	05
LACHINE	1700-1729	231	14
LACHINE	1730-1749	231	25
LACHINE	1750-1765	231	38
LACHINE	1700-1765	231	46
L'ANCIENNE LORETTE	to 1699	463	03
L'ANCIENNE LORETTE	1700-1729	463	10

L'ANCIENNE LORETTE	1730-1749	463	20
L'ANCIENNE LORETTE	1750-1765	463	33
L'ANCIENNE LORETTE	1700-1765	463	46
L'ANGE GARDIEN	to 1699	384	02
L'ANGE GARDIEN	1700-1729	384	09
L'ANGE GARDIEN	1730-1749	384	19
L'ANGE GARDIEN	1750-1765	384	32
L'ANGE GARDIEN	1700-1765	384	46
LANORAIE	1700-1765	074	46
LANORAIE	1730-1749	074	26
LANORAIE	1750-1765	074	39
LAPRAIRIE	to 1699	271	05
LAPRAIRIE	1700-1729	271	15
LAPRAIRIE	1730-1749	271	28
LAPRAIRIE	1750-1765	271	42
LAPRAIRIE	1700-1765	271	46
L'ASSOMPTION	1700-1729	284	14
L'ASSOMPTION	1730-1749	284	26
L'ASSOMPTION	1750-1765	284	39
LAVALTRIE	1730-1749	072	26
LAVALTRIE	1750-1765	072	39
LES EBOULEMENTS	1730-1749	122	19
LES EBOULEMENTS	1750-1765	122	32
LES ECUREUILS	1730-1749	446	20
LES ECUREUILS	1750-1765	446	33
L'ISLET	to 1699	311	03
L'ISLET	1700-1729	311	11
L'ISLET	1730-1749	311	21
L'ISLET	1750-1765	311	34
L'ISLET	1700-1765	311	46
LIST OF IMMIGRANTS: FAUX SAUNIERS	1700-1765	800	46
LONGUE POINTE	1700-1729	193	14
LONGUE POINTE	1730-1749	193	25
LONGUE POINTE	1750-1765	193	38
LONGUEUIL	to 1699	102	05
LONGUEUIL	1700-1729	102	15
LONGUEUIL	1730-1749	102	28
LONGUEUIL	1750-1765	102	42
LOTBINIERE	to 1699	321	03
LOTBINIERE	1700-1729	321	11
LOTBINIERE	1730-1749	321	22

LOTBINIERE	1750-1765	321	35
LOTBINIERE	1700-1765	321	46
MASCOUCHE	1750-1765	285	39
MASKINONGE	1700-1729	332	12
MASKINONGE	1730-1749	332	23
MASKINONGE	1750-1765	332	36
MISSION DE LA MONTAGNE DE MONTREAL	to 1699	394	05
MISSION DES HURONS DE LA JEUNE LORETTE	1750-1765	464	33
MISSION D'L'ILE TOURTES	to 1699	236	05
MONT LOUIS	1700-1729	185	11
MONTREAL	1700-1765	391	46
NATURALIZATIONS	1700-1765		46
NEUVILLE	to 1699	442	03
NEUVILLE	1700-1729	442	10
NEUVILLE	1730-1749	442	20
NEUVILLE	1750-1765	442	33
NICOLET	1700-1729	412	12
NICOLET	1730-1749	412	23
NICOLET	1750-1765	412	36
NOTRE DAME DE MONTREAL	to 1699	391	05
NOTRE DAME DE MONTREAL	1700-1729	391	13
NOTRE DAME DE MONTREAL	1730-1749	391	24
NOTRE DAME DE MONTREAL	1750-1765	391	37
NOTRE DAME DE QUEBEC	to 1699	451	01
NOTRE DAME DE QUEBEC	1700-1729	451	08
NOTRE DAME DE QUEBEC	1730-1749	451	18
NOTRE DAME DE QUEBEC	1750-1765	451	31
PABOS	1750-1765	182	34
PETITE RIVIERE ST FRANCOIS	1730-1749	123	19
PETITE RIVIERE ST FRANCOIS	1700-1765	123	46

POINTE AUX TREMBLES	to 1699	191	05
POINTE AUX TREMBLES	1700-1729	191	14
POINTE AUX TREMBLES	1730-1749	191	25
POINTE AUX TREMBLES	1750-1765	191	38
POINTE AUX TREMBLES	1700-1765	191	46
POINTE CLAIRE	1700-1729	233	14
POINTE CLAIRE	1730-1749	233	25
POINTE CLAIRE	1750-1765	233	38
POINTE DE LEVIS	to 1699	301	03
POINTE DE LEVIS	1700-1729	301	11
POINTE DE LEVIS	1730-1749	301	22
POINTE DE LEVIS	1750-1765	301	35
POINTE DE LEVIS	1700-1765	301	46
POINTE DU LAC	1730-1749	531	23
POINTE DU LAC	1750-1765	531	36
POINTE OLIVIER	1730-1749	491	27
POINTE OLIVIER	1750-1765	491	41
POSTES DU DOMAINE DU ROI	to 1699	501	03
POSTES DU DOMAINE DU ROI	1700-1729	501	09
POSTES DU DOMAINE DU ROI	1730-1749	501	19
POSTES DU DOMAINE DU ROI	1750-1765	501	32
POSTES DU DOMAINE DU ROI	1700-1765	501	46
QUEBEC	1700-1765	451	46
RECENSEMENT DE 1666	1666		06
RECENSEMENT DE 1667	1667		06
RECENSEMENT DE 1681	1681		06
RECENSEMENT DE 1765	1700-1765		47
RECENSEMENT DE MONT LOUIS DE 1699	to 1699	185	06
RECENSEMENT DE MONT LOUIS DE 1700	1700-1729	185	11
RECENSEMENT DE QUEBEC 1744	1730-1749	451	18
RECENSEMENT DE QUEBEC DE 1716	1700-1729	451	08
RECENSEMENT DE QUEBEC, 1762	1700-1765		47
RECENSEMENT DE TROIS RIVIERES, 1760	1700-1765		47
REINSTATED MARRIAGES	1700-1765		46
REPENTIGNY	to 1699	281	05

REPENTIGNY	1700-1729	281	14
REPENTIGNY	1730-1749	281	26
REPENTIGNY	1750-1765	281	39
RIMOUSKI	1700-1729	481	11
RIMOUSKI	1730-1749	481	21
RIMOUSKI	1750-1765	481	34
RISTIGOUCHE	1750-1765	081	34
RIVIERE DES PRAIRIES	to 1699	192	05
RIVIERE DES PRAIRIES	1700-1729	192	14
RIVIERE DES PRAIRIES	1730-1749	192	25
RIVIERE DES PRAIRIES	1750-1765	192	38
RIVIERE DU LOUP	1700-1729	331	12
RIVIERE DU LOUP	1730-1749	331	23
RIVIERE DU LOUP	1750-1765	331	36
RIVIERE OUELLE	to 1699	251	03
RIVIERE OUELLE	1700-1729	251	11
RIVIERE OUELLE	1730-1749	251	21
RIVIERE OUELLE	1750-1765	251	34
SAULT AU RECOLLET	1730-1749	195	25
SAULT AU RECOLLET	1750-1765	195	38
SAULT ST LOUIS	1700-1729	272	15
SAULT ST LOUIS	1730-1749	272	28
SAULT ST LOUIS	1750-1765	272	42
SILLERY	to 1699	461	03
SOLDATS DU REGIMENT DE CARIGNAN	to 1699	000	06
SOREL	to 1699	471	05
SOREL	1700-1729	471	15
SOREL	1730-1749	471	27
SOREL	1750-1765	471	41
SOREL	1700-1765	471	46
SOULANGES	1750-1765	561	40
ST ANNE DE BEAUPRE	to 1699	381	02
ST ANNE DE BEAUPRE	1700-1729	381	09
ST ANNE DE BEAUPRE	1730-1749	381	19
ST ANNE DE BEAUPRE	1750-1765	381	32
ST ANNE DE LA PERADE	to 1699	114	04
ST ANNE DE LA PERADE	1700-1729	114	12
ST ANNE DE LA PERADE	1730-1749	114	23
ST ANNE DE LA PERADE	1750-1765	114	36

ST ANNE DE LA PERADE	1700-1765	114	46
ST ANNE DE LA POCATIERE	1700-1729	252	11
ST ANNE DE LA POCATIERE	1730-1749	252	21
ST ANNE DE LA POCATIERE	1700-1765	252	46
ST ANNE DE LA POCATIERIE	1750-1765	252	34
ST ANNE DU BOUT DE L'ILE	to 1699	232	05
ST ANNE DU BOUT DE L'ILE	1700-1729	232	14
ST ANNE DU BOUT DE L'ILE	1730-1749	232	25
ST ANNE DU BOUT DE L'ILE	1750-1765	232	38
ST ANTOINE	1750-1765	624	41
ST ANTOINE DE TILLY	1700-1729	323	11
ST ANTOINE DE TILLY	1730-1749	323	22
ST ANTOINE DE TILLY	1750-1765	323	35
ST ANTOINE DE TILLY	1700-1765	323	46
ST AUGUSTIN	to 1699	444	03
ST AUGUSTIN	1700-1729	444	10
ST AUGUSTIN	1730-1749	444	20
ST AUGUSTIN	1750-1765	444	33
ST AUGUSTIN	1700-1765	444	46
ST CHARLES, QUEBEC	1730-1749	064	22
ST CHARLES, QUEBEC	1750-1765	064	35
ST CHARLES, MONTREAL	1730-1749	511	27
ST CHARLES, MONTREAL	1750-1765	511	41
ST CONSTANT	1750-1765	273	42
ST CROIX	1700-1729	322	11
ST CROIX	1730-1749	322	22
ST CROIX	1750-1765	322	35
ST CROIX	1700-1765	322	46
ST DENIS	1730-1749	512	27
ST DENIS	1750-1765	512	41
ST FAMILLE, I.O.	to 1699	383	02
ST FAMILLE, I.O.	1700-1729	383	09
ST FAMILLE, I.O.	1730-1749	383	19
ST FAMILLE, I.O.	1750-1765	383	32

ST FOY	to 1699	466	03
ST FOY	1700-1729	466	10
ST FOY	1730-1749	466	20
ST FOY	1750-1765	466	33
ST FOY	1700-1765	466	46
ST FRANCOIS	1730-1749	374	21
ST FRANCOIS	1750-1765	374	34
ST FRANCOIS D'ASSISE	1750-1765	043	35
ST FRANCOIS DE SALES	1700-1729	291	14
ST FRANCOIS DE SALES	1730-1749	291	26
ST FRANCOIS DE SALES	1750-1765	291	40
ST FRANCOIS DU LAC	to 1699	631	04
ST FRANCOIS DU LAC	1700-1729	631	12
ST FRANCOIS DU LAC	1730-1749	631	23
ST FRANCOIS DU LAC	1750-1765	631	36
ST FRANCOIS DU LAC	1700-1765	631	46
ST FRANCOIS, I.O.	to 1699	387	02
ST FRANCOIS, I.O.	1700-1729	387	09
ST FRANCOIS, I.O.	1730-1749	387	19
ST FRANCOIS, I.O.	1750-1765	387	32
ST FRANCOIS, I.O.	1700-1765	387	46
ST GENEVIEVE	1730-1749	235	25
ST GENEVIEVE	1750-1765	235	38
ST GENEVIEVE	1700-1765	235	46
ST GENEVIEVE DE BATISCAN	1700-1729	115	12
ST GENEVIEVE DE BATISCAN	1730-1749	115	23
ST GENEVIEVE DE BATISCAN	1750-1765	115	36
ST GENEVIEVE DE BATISCAN	1700-1765	115	46
ST JEAN, I.O.	to 1699	388	02
ST JEAN, I.O.	1700-1729	388	09
ST JEAN, I.O.	1730-1749	388	19
ST JEAN, I.O.	1750-1765	388	32
ST JEAN, I.O.	1700-1765	388	46
ST JOACHIM	to 1699	389	02
ST JOACHIM	1700-1729	389	09
ST JOACHIM	1730-1749	389	19
ST JOACHIM	1750-1765	389	32
ST JOSEPH	1730-1749	041	22
ST JOSEPH	1750-1765	041	35

ST LAURENT	1700-1729	234	14
ST LAURENT	1730-1749	234	25
ST LAURENT	1750-1765	234	38
ST LAURENT, I.O.	to 1699	385	02
ST LAURENT, I.O.	1700-1729	385	09
ST LAURENT, I.O.	1730-1749	385	19
ST LAURENT, I.O.	1750-1765	385	32
ST MARIE	1730-1749	042	22
ST MARIE	1750-1765	042	35
ST MARIE	1700-1765	042	46
ST MICHEL	to 1699	062	03
ST MICHEL	1700-1729	062	11
ST MICHEL	1730-1749	062	22
ST MICHEL	1750-1765	062	35
ST NICOLAS	to 1699	302	03
ST NICOLAS	1700-1729	302	11
ST NICOLAS	1730-1749	302	22
ST NICOLAS	1700-1765	302	46
ST OURS	1700-1729	472	15
ST OURS	1730-1749	472	27
ST OURS	1750-1765	472	41
ST PHILIPPE	1750-1765	274	42
ST PIERRE	1700-1729	375	11
ST PIERRE	1730-1749	375	21
ST PIERRE	1750-1765	375	34
ST PIERRE LES BECQUETS	1730-1749	413	23
ST PIERRE LES BECQUETS	1750-1765	413	36
ST PIERRE, I.O.	to 1699	386	02
ST PIERRE, I.O.	1700-1729	386	09
ST PIERRE, I.O.	1730-1749	386	19
ST PIERRE, I.O.	1750-1765	386	32
ST PIERRE, I.O.	1700-1765	386	46
ST REGIS	1750-1765	201	42
ST ROCH DES AULNAIES	1730-1749	312	21
ST ROCH DES AULNAIES	1750-1765	312	34
ST ROCH DES AULNAIES	1700-1765	312	46
ST ROSE	1730-1749	293	26
ST ROSE	1750-1765	293	40
ST ROSE	1700-1765	293	46

ST SULPICE	1700-1729	283	14
ST SULPICE	1730-1749	283	26
ST SULPICE	1750-1765	283	39
ST SULPICE	1700-1765	283	46
ST THOMAS	to 1699	371	03
ST THOMAS	1700-1729	371	11
ST THOMAS	1730-1749	371	21
ST THOMAS	1750-1765	371	34
ST THOMAS	1700-1765	371	46
ST VALLIER	1700-1729	063	11
ST VALLIER	1730-1749	063	22
ST VALLIER	1750-1765	063	35
ST VALLIER	1700-1765	063	46
ST VINCENT DE PAUL	1730-1749	292	26
ST VINCENT DE PAUL	1750-1765	292	40
TERREBONNE	1700-1729	591	14
TERREBONNE	1730-1749	591	26
TERREBONNE	1750-1765	591	40
TERREBONNE	1700-1765	591	46
TROIS PISTOLES	1700-1729	581	11
TROIS PISTOLES	1730-1749	581	21
TROIS PISTOLES	1750-1765	581	34
TROIS RIVIERES	to 1699	601	04
TROIS RIVIERES	1700-1729	601	12
TROIS RIVIERES	1730-1749	601	23
TROIS RIVIERES	1750-1765	601	36
TROIS RIVIERES	1700-1765	601	46
VARENNES	to 1699	622	05
VARENNES	1700-1729	622	15
VARENNES	1730-1749	622	27
VARENNES	1750-1765	622	41
VERCHERES	1700-1729	623	15
VERCHERES	1730-1749	623	27
VERCHERES	1750-1765	623	41
WITNESSES WHO TESTIFIED IN ANNULMENTS	1700-1765		46
YAMACHICHE	1700-1729	532	12
YAMACHICHE	1730-1749	532	23
YAMACHICHE	1750-1765	532	36
YAMASKA	1700-1729	633	12
YAMASKA	1730-1749	633	23
YAMASKA	1750-1765	633	36

PRDH CODES OF 17TH CENTURY OCCUPATIONS

NO	CLASS	CATEGORY	TITLE
00	LEADING CITIZENS		ADMINISTRATORS (OF NOBLE BIRTH)
00	LEADING CITIZENS		NOBILITY
00	LEADING CITIZENS		SEIGNEUR
00	LEADING CITIZENS		SQUIRE
01	LEADING CITIZENS	BOURGEOIS, MANAGERIAL	ADMINISTRATORS (NOT OF NOBLE BIRTH)
01	LEADING CITIZENS	BOURGEOIS, MANAGERIAL	BANKER, SENESCHAL
01	LEADING CITIZENS	BOURGEOIS, MANAGERIAL	CONTRACTOR, RECEIVER GENERAL
01	LEADING CITIZENS	BOURGEOIS, MANAGERIAL	HEAD OF AN ENTERPRISE
01	LEADING CITIZENS	BOURGEOIS, MANAGERIAL	LANDHOLDERS
01	LEADING CITIZENS	BOURGEOIS, MANAGERIAL	MILL-OWNER
01	LEADING CITIZENS	BOURGEOIS, MANAGERIAL	PROVOST
01	LEADING CITIZENS	BOURGEOIS, MANAGERIAL	PUBLISHER, ATTORNEY GENERAL
02	LEADING CITIZENS	CLERGY	FRIAR/CLERIC
02	LEADING CITIZENS	CLERGY	MONK/NUN
02	LEADING CITIZENS	CLERGY	PRIEST
03	LEADING CITIZENS	ARMY AND NAVY OFFICERS	ADJUTANT
03	LEADING CITIZENS	ARMY AND NAVY OFFICERS	ARMY SURGEON
03	LEADING CITIZENS	ARMY AND NAVY OFFICERS	CADET
03	LEADING CITIZENS	ARMY AND NAVY OFFICERS	CAPTAIN
03	LEADING CITIZENS	ARMY AND NAVY OFFICERS	COLONEL
03	LEADING CITIZENS	ARMY AND NAVY OFFICERS	ENSIGN
03	LEADING CITIZENS	ARMY AND NAVY OFFICERS	LIEUTANT
03	LEADING CITIZENS	ARMY AND NAVY OFFICERS	LIEUTENANT-COLONEL
03	LEADING CITIZENS	ARMY AND NAVY OFFICERS	LIEUTENANT-MAJOR
03	LEADING CITIZENS	ARMY AND NAVY OFFICERS	MAJOR
03	LEADING CITIZENS	ARMY AND NAVY OFFICERS	SERGEANT
03	LEADING CITIZENS	ARMY AND NAVY OFFICERS	SUB-LIEUTENANT
04	LEADING CITIZENS	PROFESSIONAL	ACCOUNTANT
04	LEADING CITIZENS	PROFESSIONAL	ARCHITECT
04	LEADING CITIZENS	CIVIL SERVANTS	BAILIFF
04	LEADING CITIZENS	CIVIL SERVANTS	CLERK OF THE COURT
04	LEADING CITIZENS	PROFESSIONAL	ENGINEER
04	LEADING CITIZENS	PROFESSIONAL	JUDGE
04	LEADING CITIZENS	PROFESSIONAL	LAWYER
04	LEADING CITIZENS	PROFESSIONAL	NOTARY
04	LEADING CITIZENS	CIVIL SERVANTS	PUBLIC PROSECUTOR
04	LEADING CITIZENS	CIVIL SERVANTS	SECRETARY
04	LEADING CITIZENS	PROFESSIONAL	SURVEYOR

05	LEADING CITIZENS	MEDICAL PROFESSION	APOTHECARY
05	LEADING CITIZENS	MEDICAL PROFESSION	DENTIST
05	LEADING CITIZENS	MEDICAL PROFESSION	DOCTOR OF MEDICINE
05	LEADING CITIZENS	MEDICAL PROFESSION	MIDWIFE
05	LEADING CITIZENS	MEDICAL PROFESSION	NURSE
05	LEADING CITIZENS	MEDICAL PROFESSION	OTHER SPECIALISTS
05	LEADING CITIZENS	MEDICAL PROFESSION	PHARMACIST
05	LEADING CITIZENS	MEDICAL PROFESSION	SURGEON
06	LEADING CITIZENS	TRADE	ANIMAL SELLER
06	LEADING CITIZENS	TRADE	BOOKSELLER
06	LEADING CITIZENS	TRADE	CANTEEN-KEEPER
06	LEADING CITIZENS	TRADE	GROCER/CATERER
06	LEADING CITIZENS	TRADE	HOTEL-KEEPER
06	LEADING CITIZENS	TRADE	INNKEEPER (CABARETIER)
06	LEADING CITIZENS	TRADE	QUARTERMASTER
06	LEADING CITIZENS	TRADE	SHOPKEEPER
06	LEADING CITIZENS	TRADE	TRADESMAN
07	LEADING CITIZENS	HONORARY OFFICES	ALDERMAN
07	LEADING CITIZENS	HONORARY OFFICES	CHURCHWARDEN
07	LEADING CITIZENS	HONORARY OFFICES	SYNDIC
08	LEADING CITIZENS	NON-COMM AND JR OFFICERS	CAPTAIN OF THE INHABITANTS
08	LEADING CITIZENS	NON-COMM AND JR OFFICERS	CORPORAL
08	LEADING CITIZENS	NON-COMM AND JR OFFICERS	DRUMMER, TRUMPETER
08	LEADING CITIZENS	NON-COMM AND JR OFFICERS	FENCING MASTER
08	LEADING CITIZENS	NON-COMM AND JR OFFICERS	LANCE-CORPORAL
08	LEADING CITIZENS	NON-COMM AND JR OFFICERS	QUARTERMASTER
08	LEADING CITIZENS	NON-COMM AND JR OFFICERS	QUARTERMASTER SERGEANT
08	LEADING CITIZENS	NON-COMM AND JR OFFICERS	SERGEANT
08	LEADING CITIZENS	NON-COMM MILITIAMEN	TOWN-MAJOR
09	LEADING CITIZENS	PROFESSIONAL	JOURNALIST
09	LEADING CITIZENS	PROFESSIONAL	TEACHER
10	FOOD-TRADE CRAFTSMEN		BUTCHER
10	FOOD-TRADE CRAFTSMEN		PORK BUTCHER
11	FOOD-TRADE CRAFTSMEN		BAKER
12	FOOD-TRADE CRAFTSMEN		FLOUR DEALER
12	FOOD-TRADE CRAFTSMEN		MILLER
13	FOOD-TRADE CRAFTSMEN		PASTRY COOK
14	FOOD-TRADE CRAFTSMEN		VINEGAR MAKER
15	FOOD-TRADE CRAFTSMEN		BREWER
15	FOOD-TRADE CRAFTSMEN		DISTILLER
16	FOOD-TRADE CRAFTSMEN		SALT MERCHANT

17	FOOD-TRADE CRAFTSMEN		BUTTER MAKER
17	FOOD-TRADE CRAFTSMEN		CHEESE MAKER
17	FOOD-TRADE CRAFTSMEN		DAIRYMAN
18	FOOD-TRADE CRAFTSMEN		TOBACCO MAKER
20	TEXTILE WORKERS		CARDER
20	TEXTILE WORKERS		COMBER
20	TEXTILE WORKERS		DRAW-BOY
20	TEXTILE WORKERS		SHEARER
20	TEXTILE WORKERS		SPINNER
21	TEXTILE WORKERS		HATTER
21	TEXTILE WORKERS		HOSIER
22	TEXTILE WORKERS		ROPEMAKER
23	TEXTILE WORKERS		CLOTHIER
23	TEXTILE WORKERS		SERGE MAKER
24	TEXTILE WORKERS		MASTER COUTURIER
24	TEXTILE WORKERS		MILLINER
24	TEXTILE WORKERS		SEAMSTRESS
24	TEXTILE WORKERS		TAILOR
25	TEXTILE WORKERS		WEAVER (TISSERAND)
25	TEXTILE WORKERS		WEAVER (TISSIER)
26	TEXTILE WORKERS		TAPESTRY-MAKER
26	TEXTILE WORKERS		WIGMAKER
28	TEXTILE WORKERS		BASKET MAKER
30	LEATHER CRAFTSMEN		SHOEMAKER, COBBLER
31	LEATHER CRAFTSMEN		CURRIER
32	LEATHER CRAFTSMEN		SADDLER
33	LEATHER CRAFTSMEN		CHAMOIS-DRESSER
33	LEATHER CRAFTSMEN		LEATHER WORKER
33	LEATHER CRAFTSMEN		TANNER
33	LEATHER CRAFTSMEN		TAWER
34	LEATHER CRAFTSMEN		FURRIER
39	LEATHER CRAFTSMEN		NON-SPECIALIZED CRAFTSMEN
40	BUILDER		BRICKMAKER
40	BUILDER		LIME-BURNER
41	BUILDER		CARPENTER
41	BUILDER		SHIPWRIGHT
42	BUILDER		ROOFER

43	BUILDER		MASON
44	BUILDER		HOUSE PAINTER
44	BUILDER		MONUMENTAL MASON
44	BUILDER		SAWYER
44	BUILDER		SCULPTOR
44	BUILDER		STONE-CUTTER
45	BUILDER		CAULKER
46	BUILDER		GLAZIER
50	WOODWORKERS		WHEELWRIGHT
51	WOODWORKERS		CARPENTER
52	WOODWORKERS		CLOG-MAKER
53	WOODWORKERS		CABINETMAKER
53	WOODWORKERS		TURNER
53	WOODWORKERS		WOODCARVER
54	WOODWORKERS		COOPER
60	METALWORKERS		ARMORER
60	METALWORKERS		ARMORER (SWORD)
60	METALWORKERS		ARQUEBUSIER
60	METALWORKERS		GUNNER
60	METALWORKERS		GUNSMITH
61	METALWORKERS		BUTTON MAKER
61	METALWORKERS		COPPERSMITH
61	METALWORKERS		POTTER
61	METALWORKERS		TINSMITH
62	METALWORKERS		CUTLER
62	METALWORKERS		EDGE-TOOL MAKER
62	METALWORKERS		NAILSMITH
63	METALWORKERS		BLACKSMITH
63	METALWORKERS		FARRIER
64	METALWORKERS		CASTER
64	METALWORKERS		METALWORKER
65	METALWORKERS		BINDER
65	METALWORKERS		PRINTER
65	METALWORKERS		TYPOGRAPHER
66	METALWORKERS		CLOCKMAKER
66	METALWORKERS		SILVERSMITH, GOLDSMITH
67	METALWORKERS		LOCKSMITH, IRONSMITH

68	METALWORKERS		MECHANIC
68	METALWORKERS		WORKER IN LEAD
70	FARMERS AND BREEDERS		FARMER
70	FARMERS AND BREEDERS		HABITANT
70	FARMERS AND BREEDERS		WINE GROWER
71	FARMERS AND BREEDERS		UNDECLARED HABITANT (CENSUS)
72	FARMERS AND BREEDERS		FARMER
73	FARMERS AND BREEDERS		HIRED MAN
73	FARMERS AND BREEDERS		JOURNEYMAN
74	FARMERS AND BREEDERS		COLONIST
74	FARMERS AND BREEDERS		SETTLER
75	FARMERS AND BREEDERS		PLOWMAN, HUSBANDMAN
76	FARMERS AND BREEDERS		DIGGER
76	FARMERS AND BREEDERS		GARDENER
76	FARMERS AND BREEDERS		HORTICULTURIST
76	FARMERS AND BREEDERS		MARKET GARDENER
77	FARMERS AND BREEDERS		BREEDER
78	FARMERS AND BREEDERS		FISHERMAN
79	FARMERS AND BREEDERS		STOCK-FARMER
80	SERVANTS		APPRENTICE
80	SERVANTS		CLERK
80	SERVANTS		COACHMAN
80	SERVANTS		COOK
80	SERVANTS		DOMESTIC
80	SERVANTS		GROOM, OSTLER
80	SERVANTS		MAIDSERVANT
80	SERVANTS		VALET
81	SERVANTS		HOUSEKEEPER
81	SERVANTS		INTENDANT OF A LORD/BOURGEOIS
81	SERVANTS		LADY'S COMPANION
81	SERVANTS		LADY'S MAID, BUTLER
82	SERVANTS		BONDSMAN
83	SERVANTS		CLEANER
83	SERVANTS		DRYER
83	SERVANTS		LAUNDERER
84	SERVANTS		CARTER
84	SERVANTS		FERRYMAN
84	SERVANTS		HAULER
84	SERVANTS		WAGONER

85	SERVANTS		APPRENTICE (FIELD UNMENTIONED)
85	SERVANTS		MESSENGER
86	SERVANTS		COURIER
86	SERVANTS		POST-HORSE
86	SERVANTS		POSTILION
86	SERVANTS		POSTMAN
86	SERVANTS		USHER
87	SERVANTS		BEADLER, CANTOR
87	SERVANTS		CUSTOMS OFFICER
87	SERVANTS		FIREMAN
87	SERVANTS		GUARD, KEEPER
87	SERVANTS		JAILER
87	SERVANTS		OVERSEER
88	SERVANTS	OFFICER-WORKERS	CLERK
88	SERVANTS	OFFICER-WORKERS	COFFEE-BEARER
88	SERVANTS	OFFICER-WORKERS	COPYIST
89	SERVANTS	ARTISTS	ACTOR
89	SERVANTS	ARTISTS	MUSICIAN
89	SERVANTS	ARTISTS	PAINTER
89	SERVANTS	ARTISTS	SCULPTOR
90	LABOURERS		GARRISON SOLDIER
90	LABOURERS		MILITIAMAN
90	LABOURERS		REGULAR
90	LABOURERS		SOLDIER, GUARDSMAN
91	LABOURERS	SEAFARERS	HELMSMAN
91	LABOURERS	SEAFARERS	MASTER
91	LABOURERS	SEAFARERS	PILOT
91	LABOURERS	SEAFARERS	SAIL MAKER
91	LABOURERS	SEAFARERS	SAILOR
91	LABOURERS	SEAFARERS	SEAMAN
91	LABOURERS	SEAFARERS	SHIP'S BOY
92	LABOURERS		BLOCK-MAKER
92	LABOURERS		CHARCOAL BURNER
92	LABOURERS		DOCKER
92	LABOURERS		HEWER
92	LABOURERS		LABOURER
92	LABOURERS		MINER
92	LABOURERS		SWEEP
92	LABOURERS		WORKER
92	LABOURERS		WORKHAND
93	LABOURERS		GUNPOWDER MAKER
93	LABOURERS		TALLOW CHANDLER
94	LABOURERS		DRIVER
94	LABOURERS		LUMBERJACK
94	LABOURERS		PIT SAWYER

94	LABOURERS		WOODCUTTER
95	LABOURERS		COWHERD
95	LABOURERS		HERDSMAN
95	LABOURERS		SHEPHERD
95	LABOURERS		SWINEHERD
96	LABOURERS		COUREUR DE BOIS
96	LABOURERS		FARMER OF REVENUE, OF TAXES
96	LABOURERS		HUNTER
96	LABOURERS		INTERPRETER
96	LABOURERS		TRAPPER, FUR TRADER
96	LABOURERS		VOYAGEUR
97	LABOURERS		BEGGAR
97	LABOURERS		VAGABOND
98	LABOURERS		DEALER IN CONTRABAND SALT
98	LABOURERS		DEFRAUDER
98	LABOURERS		POACHER
98	LABOURERS		PRISONER
98	LABOURERS		SMUGGLER
99	LABOURERS		UNEMPLOYED

BAPTISM, MARRIAGE AND BURIAL RECORDS

Baptism, Marriage, and Burial Records

The baptism, marriage and burial records of most of the parishes of Quebec have been published over the years.

These are also called repertoires, meaning "a listing of many items". Most of these published records start with the beginning of the parish and end at some year in the current century. They might include only marriages, only baptisms, or only burials, or they might include all three categories. They are usually published by the parishes, or by genealogical or historical societies. Many times the publication is prompted by a special anniversary of the parish. Many of them are out of print.

There are references in print that list all of the published records.

Most volumes include information on one specific parish. A few volumes however combine information on a number of parishes. In this case, each of the listings will include a reference to which parish the event occurred in. This is usually in abbreviated form and you will need to consult the table of abbreviations in the front of the volume

Most of the formats of these repertoires are very similar, and are fairly easy to understand with a little practice and patience. Some important items to remember are:

Dates are usually in the form (DD/MM/YYYY) where D=Day, M=Month, and Y=year.

"X" or "f" means deceased. "f" stands for the French word "feu" which means late or deceased.

"Veuf" means "widower of".

"Veuve" means "widow of".

The following are examples of what you might find in any of them.

Baptismal Records

Most records are in alphabetical order by surname. The next sorting is either alphabetically by first name or chronologically by date of baptism. The following is a sample of one entry in the baptismal records of St-Pierre-de-Sorel.

1825-01-11	01-10	ANTAYA Paul	Michel	Josephte DUPRE
1.	**2.**	**3.**	**4.**	**5.**

1. Date of baptism.
2. Date of birth. Year 1825 is assumed.
3. Name of baptised. Surname in upper case.
4. Fisrt name of father. Last name is assumed to be ANTAYA.
5. Mother's full name. Surname in upper case.

Here is another example from the parish of L'Epiphanie.

	1.	**2.**	**3.**	**4.**
AMIREAULT	M. Gisele Lise	Lucien	cultivateur,	Albertine Lussier
1876-09-18	09-18	(J. Edouard Amirault grand-pere, M. Louise Magnan son espouse)		
5.	**6.**	**7.**		

1. Name of baptised. Surname in upper case.
2. Name of father. Last name is assumed to be Amireault.
3. Occupation. (Farmer).
4. Name of mother.
5. Date of baptism.
6. Date of birth. Year 1876 is assumed.
7. Name(s) of godparents or witnesses.
   (J. Edward Amirault, grandfather and his spouse, M. Louise Magnan).

Notice again that the surname of the father is not given and is assumed to be the same as the surname of the individual baptised. This same rule holds true for the year of birth.

Marriage Records

Marriage records are usually printed in alphabetical order by surname of the husband. The next sorting is usually alphabetical by first name of husband. Sometimes you will find the second sorting to be alphabetical by the surname of the wife. This can facilitate your search if you are not sure of the first name of the husband or if there are many entries with the same name. For example, if you are searching for the marriage of Joseph COLUMBE to Dorilda BEAULIEU, you might find that there are 15 entries for the name Joseph COLUMBE. Your next step should be to quickly scan the list of wife's surnames for the surname BEAULIEU.

Similar to baptismal records, publications of marriage records are usually done for specific parishes. However, there are some volumes that include the parishes of entire counties or regions. In this case each entry will show an abbreviation for the parish and you will usually have to refer to the listing of parish abbreviations in the front of the volume.

The information shown in a marriage record might include some or all of the following:

- Name of Husband Name of Wife

- Name of husband's parents Name of wife's parents

- Whether or not the parents are living or deceased

- The parish or prior place of residence of the spouse, if different from the site of the marriage.

- The parish or place of residence of the parents.

(Note: these last two items of information are very important because it could lead you to find additional family members in other parishes).

- Whether or not either of the spouses were widowed, and if so, the name of the prior spouse. If this is the case, then the parents of the widowed spouse are not shown.

The following is an extract from the marriage records of Ste-Elisabeth, Comte de Berthier.

1.	2.	3.
ROUSSEAU Jean-Bte (St Thomas)	03-11-1852	MIVILLE-DECHENE Thersile
Jean-Bte et Sophie Dubord-Lafontaine (St Cuthbert)		Michel et Marie Ouellet
4.		**5.**

1. Name of husband. Surname in upper case. His parish in parentheses.
2. Date of marriage.
3. Name of wife. Surname in upper case.
4. Names of parents of husband and their parish.
5. Names of parents of wife.

Next is an example from the marriage records of St-Barthelemy in Berthier County. This entire entry was on one line in the publication. The "x" means deceased.

1.	2.	3.	4.	5.
CARON Charles	S. David	(x Ambroise, Marie Luneau)	S. Cuthbert	1838-02-13
	MENARD Marie	(x Louis, x Therese Lavanture)	S.Gen. Berthier	
	6.		**7.**	**8.**

1. Name of husband. Surname in upper case.
2. His parish — St-David.
3. Names of his parents. Ambroise, the father, is deceased. His surname is assumed to be that of his son. The mother is Marie Luneau.
4. The parish of the parents — St-Cuthbert.
5. The date of marriage.
6. The name of the wife.
7. Names of the wife's parents.
8. Parish of the parents — Ste-Genevieve, Berthier.

Burial Records

Published burial records include some or all of the following information.

Name of the decedent.
Occupation of decedent.
Date of burial.
Date of death.
Age at time of death.
Name of spouse, or
Name of parents.
Name of witnesses.
Relation of witnesses.
Occupation of witnesses.

Important items to remember include the following.

"s" is the abbreviation for the French word "sépulture",
   which means "burial".

"a" is the abbreviation for the French word "année" which means "year".

"m" is the abbreviation for the French word "mois" which means "month".

"ondoye" is French for "baptized at home" or "privately baptized". This reference is usually found when the child died on or near the date of birth. In the early days, the priest was usually not available to baptize immediately upon birth, and so, if the child was in danger of death, the baptism was performed by a parent or relative.

"Anonyme" is French for "unnamed". This is usually shown at a stillbirth or the death of a child shortly after birth.

"fille" is French for "girl".   "garçon" is French for "boy".

"naissant" is French for "new-born".

"époux" is French for "husband".   "épouse" is French for "wife".

The following are examples of burial records from two different publications.

1.		2.
LAFOREST Remi cultivateur		epoux Denise Berard
1896-11-21 -11-18 (Age: 27a.)		(Pierre Laforest pere, ses freres Louis, Alfred, Baptiste et Joseph)
3. **4.** **5.**		**6.**

1. Name of decedent (Remi LAFOREST) & occupation (cultivateur = farmer).
2. Name of spouse. (Husband of Denise Berard).
3. Date of burial.
4. Date of death. Year 1896 is assumed.
5. Age at death. (27 years old).
6. Indiviuals present at the burial. (His father, Pierre, and his 4 brothers).

Here is another example.

1.	2.	3.
ASSELIN Anonyme fille ondoyee	Hector, Doria Laferriere (ondoyee par Dr. Pelletier)	
1923-02-25 02-24	(Hector Asselin, Hector Laferriere)	
4. **5.**	**6.**	

1. Name of decendent. (Unnamed girl, baptised at home).
2. Names of parents. (Hector is the father, last name assumed to be ASSELIN. Doria Laferriere is the mother).
3. Baptised by Dr. Pelletier.
4. Date of burial.
5. Date of death. Year 1923 assumed.
6. Witnesses at the burial.

THE LOISELLE INDEX

THE LOISELLE INDEX

The Loiselle Index is a voluminous work, widely known in genealogical circles, and currently preserved at the National Archives of Québec at Québec.

One man, Rev. Antonin Loiselle, is responsible for this magnificent effort.

A Dominican Priest, Father Loiselle began collecting information on French-Canadian marriages as he traveled to different parishes. Starting in about 1930 and working through the next 20 years, he accumulated, and printed on index cards, approximately 1,100,000 marriages taken from the registers of the Catholic parishes of 15 of the dioceses of Québec, Madwaska, and Eastern Ontario. Fr. Loiselle died in Laval in 1986.

The Loiselle Card Index was housed at the Québec National Archives in 1963 and was made available to the general public for research. After more than 20 years of regular daily public use, the Archives decided to collaborate with the Genealogical Society of Québec in the task of rearranging, refiling and, in general, reorganizing the cards, to facilitate research.

Many years earlier, the Mormon Family History Library had microfilmed the collection and the microfilm had been available for research at the various libraries. Now a decision was made to film the entire collection on microfiche in order to make it available to a much larger audience.

A project of this magnitude could not have been accomplished without the help of a great number of volunteers from the Genealogical Society and the helpful assistance of the staff at the Archives. This microfiche collection stands in testimony to their efforts and those efforts should be applauded by the entire French-Canadian genealogical community.

The reorganizing of a card index so voluminous would not have been successful if various filing criteria had not first been established.

The following are some of the concerns that were raised and discussed prior to settling upon the agreed-to filing method.

A number of similar card indices already existed which were sorted alphabetically by the surname of the husband.

Numerous marriage repertoires had been published utilizing various methods of indexing.

After polling many of the individual users of the Loiselle Index, it was decided to file the cards in alphabetical order by the surnames of each of the spouses.

Filing the cards by male names in the first section and by female names in the second section would cut down significantly on the time it would take to research.

And so the cards of the men and the cards of the women were separated and placed in two independent sections. These sections were then alphabetized by surname. (Item 1 on the index card) (Refer to Figure 10-1 on page 4)

Cards with the same surname were then place in alphabetical order by the surname of the spouse. (Item 3 on the index card)

Cards with same surname of the spouse were then filed in alphabetical order by the first name. (Item 4 on the index card)

If 1, 3, and 4, were identical, then the cards were filed chronologically by date of marriage. (Item 5 on the index card)

During the course of the filing and preparing the index for microfilming, several problems were encountered, the understanding of which will benefit the user.

If an individual has two names, the card will be filed under the first of those names. For instance Jean Hudon - Beaulieu will be filed under Hudon.

Cross-references to related surnames, as well as spelling variations, are shown on the index card dividers. For example, Aler, Allaire, Haller or Beauche, Baucher, Boscher.

Another important thing to understand is that all variations of a recognized surname are filed within the order of the main variation without regard to their spellings. For example, Moricet, Morisset, and Morisette will be filed together under the most common of those names.

If the card for an individual identifies the spouse only by a first name then that card will be filed in alphabetical order, first by the surname of the individual, then by the first name of the spouse. If the spouse is anonymous the same rule will apply.

Saint/Sainte or St/Ste surnames are filed in the "Sa" section without regard to whether they are the masculine or feminine version.

During this undertaking, hundreds of cards were found to contain comments written in by some of the prior researchers. The team of volunteers conducted extensive additional research in an attempt to justify these comments. Certain of these cases were not solvable, but the comments were left in just on the chance that they might provide some additional clues to future researchers.

Many cards were too damaged or contained too much information to be microfilmed and so they were copied over.

The cards for the Therrien family were found to be missing entirely . Thanks to Mr. Leo Therrien, his personal card index of the Therriens is included at the end of the alphabet, in each section - men and women.

1,000 newspaper clippings were pasted to the backs of file cards by Father Loiselle and by other researchers eager to add information to the file. These cards were photocopied and then filed in their normal alphabetical order within the index.

These newsclippings are full of additional information and original news, such as, deaths, ages, places of residence and burial, family relationships, professions, circumstances of death, social implications, lawsuits, and some biographies.

Whether the information on the clipping had to do with a man or a woman, the entire file of clippings was filed alphabetically and placed in the appendix to each section.

The following page contains an enlarged example of what you will find on one of the Loiselle Index Cards (Figure 10-1).

LOISELLE INDEX CARD - MICROFICHE

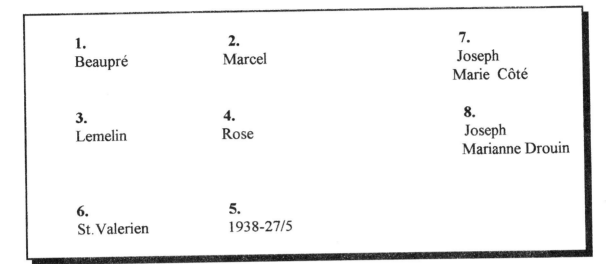

1. Beaupré	**2.** Marcel	**7.** Joseph Marie Côté
3. Lemelin	**4.** Rose	**8.** Joseph Marianne Drouin
6. St. Valerien	**5.** 1938-27/5	

Figure 10-1

Definitions:

1. The family name or surname of the individual who is the object of this card.

2. His first name or given name.

3. The family name or surname of the spouse.

4. The first name or given name of the spouse.

5. The date of marriage. It is in the form: year -day/month.

6. The place of the marriage.

7. The names of the parents of the individual who is the object of this card.

8. The names of the parents of the spouse.

COMMON TERMS AND ABBREVIATIONS

Abbreviations Used in French-Canadian Genealogy

FRENCH	ENGLISH
abrége son nom et s'apelle L'arche	abbreviated his name to L'arche
allant en canot aux Trois-Rivières	going to Trois-Rivières by canoe
ancien soldat	former soldier
anglais de nation	Englishman
anonyme	anonymous
appélée...du nom de sa mère	goes by...his mother's name
armurier	gun maker
arpenteur	land surveyor
arquebusier	rifleman
arrivé au canada	arrived in Canada
aussi appélée Louise	also known as Louise
aux registres de la paroisse	according to the parish registers
avec dispense	with dispensation
avec dispense du 2e au 2e degré	dispensed from 2nd degree of affinity
b. or baptême	baptism
barque	boat
basque de nation	of the Basque nationality
beau-frère	brother-in-law
beau-père	father-in-law
bedeau	church sexton
belle-mère	mother-in-law
belle-soeur	sister-in-law
bombardier	bombardier (military)

FRENCH	ENGLISH
boucher	butcher
boulanger	baker
bourgeois	merchant
brasseur	brewer
briquetier	brick maker
brulé en 1690 par les iroquois	burned (at the stake) in 1690 by the Iroquois
cannonier	cannoner (military)
captaine de vaisseau	ship's captain
capitaine de milice	captain of the militia
caporal	corporal (military)
chapelier	hat maker
charbonnier	coal merchant
charpentier	carpenter
charpentier de navire	ship's carpenter
charron	wheel maker
chaudonnier	coppersmith, pot maker
chirurgien	surgeon
commis	shop clerk
connue sous le nom ...	known under the name of ...
contrat de mariage	marriage contract
contremaitre du vaisseau	petty officer (military)
cordonnier	shoemaker
cousins germains	first cousins

FRENCH	ENGLISH
coutelier	knife maker
cuisinier	cook
de ce mariage sont nés...	of this marriage were born...
d. or décédé	died
déclaré nul	declared null and void
défricheur	land clearer
demeurant	living in (at)
dit	so called, also known as, alias
domestique	house servant (female)
domicilié	living at (in)
drapier	cloth merchant
du 49ème régiment	from the 49th regiment (military)
elle épouse...	she married...
élu marguillier	elected churchwarden
en sauvage: Kil8abé	the Indian name is Kil8abe (pronounced *kill-wheat-ah-bay*). As there is no French alphabet equivalent to the particular sound between the Indian name Kil and abé, the French used the number 8, "huit" ,to indicate the closest sound. This sound is closely equivalent to the English word "wheat".
enfant de nourrice	a baby who is being nursed
engagé	hired hand (under contract)
esclave	slave
étranger a la paroisse	unknown in this parish
évêque	bishop
excommunieé	excommunicated

FRENCH	ENGLISH
fait prisonnier de guerre	made prisoner of war
farinier	flour merchant
fermier	farmer
fille adonptive	adopted (f)
fils adoptif	adopted (m)
garçon engagé	hired hand (m)
gouverneur	governor
grand'mere	grandmother
greffier	court clerk
grenadier	grenadier (military)
habitant	inhabitant
huissier	public official
il épouse...	he married...
il était...	he was...
imbécille	imbecile (f.)
ingenieur	engineer
inhumé	buried
interprète	interpreter or translator
jardinier	gardener
journalier	day laborer
juge	judge

FRENCH	ENGLISH
jumeaux	twins (males)
jumelles	twins (females)
laboureur	laborer (farm worker)
le nom manque au registre	the name is missing in the register
le véritable nom est...	the actual name is ...
lieutenant	lieutenant (military)
maçon	mason, stone cutter
maître armurier	master gun maker
maître boucher	master butcher
maître boulanger	master baker
maître calfateur	master boat caulker
maître charpentier de navire	master ship's carpenter
maître chirugien	master surgeon
maître cordonnier	master shoemaker
maitre de barque	ship's captain
majeur	a male who is of legal age to marry
major	major (military)
manoeuvre	unskilled workman
marchand	merchant
marié sous le nom de Rivet	married under the name of Rivet
marraine	godmother

FRENCH	ENGLISH
matelot	sailor
maure de nation	of the Moorish nationality
menusier	cabinet maker
métayer	tenant farmer
meunier au moulin	miller
milice	militiaman
milicien canadien	Canadian militiaman
mineure	a female who is of legal age to marry
mort dans le bois	died in the forest (probably cutting wood)
mouleur	blacksmith
moulin a fariné	grist mill
musicien	musician
n. or naissance	birth
natif de ...	native of ...
notaire	notary
notaire public	notary public
noyé dans la rade	found drowned by the roadside
panis(e) de nation	of the Panis nation (one of the many Indian nations)
parraine	godfather
pas marié	not married

FRENCH	ENGLISH
passé contrat de mariage	signed a marriage contract
patissier	pastry cook
pauvre mendiant	indigent (homeless pauper)
pilot	ship's pilot
prêtre	priest
pris dans une attrappe à ours	caught in a bear trap (ouch!)
pris	taken
procès-verbaux	testimony
procureur fiscal	tax collector
recensement	census
réhabilitation	rehabilitation. Solemnifying a marriage in the Catholic Church that had previously been performed in either a non-Catholic ceremony or a marriage performed before a justice-of-the-peace.
réhabilité	same as rehabilitation
réligieuse	nun
s. or sepulture	burial
sacristan	church warden
sage-femme	mid-wife
scieur	wood sawer
second femme	second wife
second maître	second mate

FRENCH	ENGLISH
sellier	saddle maker
sergent	sergeant (military)
serrurier	locksmith
servant	gunner
serviteur	servant
soldat dans le ... régiment	soldier in the ... regiment
soldat de la garnison	garrison soldier
soldat	soldier
taillandier	maker of cutting tools
tailleur d'habits	tailor
tambour major	drum major (military)
tambourineur	drummer (military)
tanneur	leather tanner
tisserand	weaver
tixier	spinner of wool
tonnelier	barrel maker
travailleur	laborer
trouvé gelé	found frozen
trouvé noyé au rivage	found drowned on the river bank

FRENCH	ENGLISH
tué d'une chute de cheval	died from a fall from a horse
tué par les anglais	killed by the English
tué par les iroquois	killed by the Iroquois
valet	servant
variations et surnom	variations and surnames
vénu	came
vénu en 1758	came in 1758
voy. or voyez	see

Abbreviations - Add Your Own

FRENCH	ENGLISH

FRENCH-CANADIAN GENEALOGICAL TIMELINE

French-Canadian Research Timeline

Source	to 1699	1725	1750	1775	1800	1825	1850	1875	1900	1925	1950	1975	post 1975

TANGUAY 1630 - 1760   7 Volumes   *Genealogies*
Dictionnaire genealogique des familles canadiennes

DROUIN 1608 - 1760   3 Volumes   *Marriage Records*
Dictionnaire national des Canadiens français

JETTÉ 1621 - 1730   1 Volume   *Genealogies*
Dictionnaire généalogique des familles du Québec

PRDH 1621 - 1765   47 Volumes   *Baptism, Marriage, Burial, and Census Records*
Le Répertoire des actes de baptême, mariage, sépulture et des recensements du Québec ancien

LOISELLE INDEX 1608 - 1963   *Marriage Records*
Marriages by Name of Bride and Groom   Microfilm (174 reels) and Microfiche

BAPTISM, MARRIAGE, AND BURIAL RECORDS - GENERAL
The most common are marriage records published by parish.   Covers period from the start of the parish to date of publication.

RIVEST INDEX   1608 - 1972   *Marriage Records*
Marriages by Name of Bride - Microfilm (41 reels)

ARSENAULT   6 Volumes   *Genealogies*
History and Genealogy of the Acadians   1604 - 1755

DENISSEN   2 Volumes   *Genealogies*
French Families of the Detroit River Region 1701 - 1936

LAREAU / COURTEAU   1608 - 1979   8 Volumes   *Genealogies*
French-Canadian Families of the North Central States: A Genealogical Dictionary

DROUIN   1760 - 1935   113 Volumes   *Marriage Records*
Répertoire alphabétiques des mariages des canadiens-français

Find the date or period you are researching then draw an imaginary line from the date at the top to the bottom of the page. The references that the line intersects with are the ones that you should consider researching in first , depending upon your specific need and the geographical area.